YOUNG LION

RAHEEM
STERLING

YOUNG LION
RAHEEM STERLING

TOM AND MATT OLDFIELD

DINO

Published by Dino Books,
an imprint of John Blake Publishing Ltd,
3 Bramber Court, 2 Bramber Road,
London W14 9PB, England

www.johnblakebooks.co.uk

www.facebook.com/johnblakebooks
twitter.com/jblakebooks

This edition published in 2015

ISBN: 978 1 78418 646 3

All rights reserved. No part of this publication may be reproduced, stored in a retrieval system, or transmitted in any form or by any means, without the prior permission in writing of the publisher, nor be otherwise circulated in any form of binding or cover other than that in which it is published and without a similar condition including this condition being imposed on the subsequent purchaser.

British Library Cataloguing-in-Publication Data:

A catalogue record for this book is available from the British Library.

Design by www.envydesign.co.uk
Cover illustration by Dan Leydon
Background image Shutterstock

Printed in Great Britain by CPI Group (UK) Ltd

5 7 9 10 8 6

© Text copyright Tom and Matt Oldfield 2015

The right of Tom and Matt Oldfield to be identified as the authors of this work has been asserted by them in accordance with the Copyright, Designs and Patents Act 1988.

Papers used by John Blake Publishing are natural, recyclable products made from wood grown in sustainable forests. The manufacturing processes conform to the environmental regulations of the country of origin.

Every attempt has been made to contact the relevant copyright-holders, but some were unobtainable. We would be grateful if the appropriate people could contact us.

To Mum and Dad

For all those mornings and afternoons on the touchline, and for making all of this possible.

Also by Tom and Matt Oldfield:

Wayne Rooney: Captain of England

Gareth Bale: The Boy Who Became a Galáctico

Cover illustration by Dan Leydon.
To learn more about Dan visit danleydon.com
To purchase his artwork visit etsy.com/shop/footynews
Or just follow him on Twitter @danleydon

TABLE OF CONTENTS

ACKNOWLEDGEMENTS

This was a very special opportunity for us, as brothers, to work together on something we are both so passionate about. Football has always been a big part of our lives. We hope this book will inspire others to start/continue playing football and chasing their dreams.

Writing a book like this was one of our dreams, and we are extremely thankful to John Blake Publishing and Anna Marx, in particular, for making this project possible. Anna's guidance and patience were huge factors in our writing process.

We are also grateful to all the friends and family that encouraged us along the way. Your interest and sense of humour helped to keep us on track. Will, Doug, Mills, John, James Pang-Oldfield and the rest of our King Edward VI friends, our aunts, uncles, cousins, the Nottingham and Montreal families and so many others – thank you all.

Melissa, we could not have done this without your understanding and support. Thank you for being as excited about this collaboration as we were.

Noah, we're already doing our best to make football your favourite sport! We look forward to reading this book with you in the years ahead.

Mum and Dad, the biggest thank you is reserved for you. You introduced us to football and then devoted hours and hours to taking us to games. You bought the tickets, the kits, the boots. We love football because you encouraged us to. Thank you for all the love, all the laughs and for always believing in us. This book is for you.

CHAPTER 1

A DREAM COME TRUE

It was 14 November 2012. This was the biggest
day of Raheem's life so far – after all, you only made
your England debut once. Two months earlier, he
had been called up for the World Cup 2014 qualifier
against Ukraine and named as a substitute. He
didn't get to come on but he still learned a lot from
training with the country's best players. It was hard
watching from the bench, especially when the team
was losing with ten minutes to go. With his pace and
skill, Raheem knew he could have made a difference
on the wing against a tired defence but in the end,
England managed to get a draw without him.

This time, though, in Sweden, not only was
Raheem playing but he was starting. 'I'll be testing
some of the younger players in tomorrow's friendly,'
Roy Hodgson, the England manager, had told him
as they walked off the training pitch the day before.
'You'll be starting, Raheem – we believe you're
ready for this.' Roy had always had great faith in
him; at Liverpool, he had given him his debut at the
age of just fifteen. Raheem could only nod and flash
his trademark big smile. It was the news he'd been
waiting for.

In the tunnel before the match in Stockholm, he
took a deep breath and let the noise of the 50,000
fans in the stadium fire him up. This was what he
was born to do. Moments later, he walked out onto
the pitch, holding the hand of a Swedish mascot.
Just like for Liverpool, Steven Gerrard was there
with him as captain and mentor. In the dressing
room before the game, Stevie could see that
Raheem was nervous.

'There's nothing to worry about, kid. It's no
different to playing in front of the Kop at Liverpool.

Don't rush things today – just do your thing and enjoy it. Something tells me this won't be your only England cap!'

Stevie patted him on the back and left him to his pre-match stretches. It was a real comfort to have such experienced teammates alongside him – these big games could be pretty scary for a seventeen-year-old.

As the national anthem played, Raheem looked down proudly at the famous three lions on his white tracksuit top. He still couldn't quite believe that he was wearing the England shirt so soon into his career. What a year 2012 had been and there was still a month of it to go. Despite being born in Jamaica, England was certainly Raheem's footballing home. His homeland would always have a special place in his heart but it was in London and Liverpool that he had developed as both a player and a person.

Just before kick-off, another Liverpool teammate, Glen Johnson, came over to give him some words of advice: 'Raheem, stay focused today. You're on the right wing and I'm at right back so we'll be working together a lot. Make those amazing attacking runs when you can but don't forget to defend too. I don't want to spend the whole game clearing up your mess!' Glen gave him a friendly slap on the back and they took up their positions ready for the start.

Raheem knew it wouldn't be an easy game; the Sweden team included experienced Premier-League players like Jonas Olsson and Seb Larsson, plus one of his favourite players in the world, the amazing striker Zlatan Ibrahimović. Raheem was really looking forward to playing against Zlatan and seeing his tricks and flicks up close. Zlatan did not disappoint, scoring the first goal after 20 minutes.

Five minutes later, Raheem found space for the first time in the match and he ran at the Swedish defence before passing to Danny Welbeck, who nearly set up a goal. Raheem could sense the Sweden fans holding their breath when he had the ball at his feet. They knew he was a threat and that gave him confidence.

Raheem was involved again as England made it 1-1. Stevie passed to him deep inside his own half and this time, rather than dribbling, he did what coaches had always told him to do – 'get your head up and look up for the pass'. He could see Ashley Young making a great run over on the left and he played a great ball out to him. Ashley did brilliantly and crossed for Danny to score.

England took the lead before half-time but the second half was all about Zlatan. His second goal was a volley, his third was a powerful free-kick and his fourth was one of the best goals Raheem had ever seen, an impossible overhead kick from thirty yards out. Watching such an amazing performance, Raheem was sure that he had the desire and the talent to be that good. He just needed to keep working hard.

With five minutes to go, Raheem was substituted. 'Well done, lad,' Roy said as he made his way off the pitch. As he took his seat on the bench, Raheem felt really tired but pleased with the way he had played. It hadn't been the dream debut he had hoped for but it had been an amazing experience to represent his country. He couldn't wait to do it again, especially back at Wembley. As a kid, he had lived around the corner from the new stadium, playing football in the streets as it was being built. To play on that pitch in front of all those fans would be unbelievable.

On the flight back to England, Raheem thought back on how far he'd come. There were times when his future had looked bleak. But thanks to football, he stayed out of trouble and learnt respect, hard work and self-esteem. He owed a lot of people for the support they had given him over the years – his mum Nadine, his teachers, his coaches. They had all believed in his talent.

Most of all, he thought about what Chris, his teacher at Vernon House, had once said to him. 'If you carry on the way you're going, by the time you're seventeen you'll either be in prison or playing for England.' Raheem smiled to himself; thankfully, he had achieved the second option. But he promised himself that this was just the beginning.

CHAPTER 2

JAMAICAN SUNSHINE

It was a special vase. One that had been handed
down from generation to generation, dusted regularly
and placed proudly on a shelf in the main room. The
ball bounced up, almost in slow motion, and just
missed the vase. But it still made the shelf shake.

'How many times have I told you, Raheem?' his
grandmother yelled as she stormed into the room. 'No
football in the house! The sun is shining. Find your
friends and take the game outside.' She shook her
head as she pointed towards the back door.

Raheem knew all about that rule. But he couldn't
help it. He was only five years old and he had a lot
of energy.

He looked at the floor to show that he felt bad about nearly breaking the vase. 'I'm sorry,' he mumbled. 'I won't do it again.'

Then he raced outside into the bright sunshine, carrying the ripped ball that had almost got him in big trouble.

At the corner of the street, he saw one of his friends, Christopher. He waved. 'Want to play?'

Christopher smiled. This wasn't the first time that he had seen Raheem rush outside looking a little guilty. It usually meant that his friend had caused damage in the house by kicking the ball too hard.

'Sure. Let's ask Leon and Ridley as well. I'll get some of my dad's paint cans to use as goalposts.'

Just like that, the game was underway. That was the beauty of living in Jamaica. Raheem never had to worry about the weather. It was almost always sunny.

Even at such a young age, Raheem and his friends knew all about 'scrimmage', which was a popular style of football on the island. The goals were small and the rules were non-existent. It was a game for 'showmen', where skills were encouraged above all else. Scoring goals was still important but performing magic with the ball was encouraged even more.

Raheem had already earned a reputation among his friends in Maverley, part of the Jamaican capital of Kingston. He was skilful and competitive, but most of all he was very fast. It was almost unfair on the other boys. Raheem would just kick the ball ahead and sprint after it. No one could catch him.

'Come on, give us a chance,' Christopher complained after Raheem did his usual trick the first time he got the ball.

Raheem grinned. 'Catch me if you can!'

When he got bored of scoring goals that way, he showed off his skills. Flicks and tricks, he called it. It never took long for his friends to shout at him when he didn't let them touch the ball. 'Stop showing off, Raheem. Pass it!'

It rarely made a difference. The next minute, Raheem would be flicking the ball over a defender's head – a move known in Jamaica as a 'pile' – or knocking the ball through a defender's legs – known as a 'salad'. He was just a natural for the scrimmage style of play.

He knew all the neighbours. Some of them came out to watch the boys playing in the street, relaxing with a beer and cheering every goal. Raheem was everyone's favourite – 'dynamite', they called him.

That night, Raheem limped back into the house, exhausted from nearly two hours of football without even a five-minute break. His grandmother smiled as he wiped the sweat from his forehead. She poured him a glass of water. 'Where do you get all that energy from? It makes me tired just watching you rushing around. Wash your hands and sit down. Dinner will be on the table in two minutes.'

When his plate was placed in front of him, Raheem's eyes lit up. It was fish and potatoes, his favourite. 'Wow, you didn't tell me we were having *this*. I scored ten goals in our game this afternoon, so I think I earned it!'

His grandmother winked at him. Then her face turned more serious. 'Well, you might not have been getting any dinner at all if you'd broken that vase.'

Raheem went red, imagining how that conversation might have gone. He loved his grandmother. She was funny and always took good care of her grandchildren, but she was scary when she got angry.

After dinner, he helped bring the plates and glasses into the kitchen. While his grandmother stood at the sink, Raheem asked, 'Did we get any post today?'

His grandmother turned off the tap and turned to face Raheem, with a sympathetic look. 'Not today. But your mum is going to send another letter soon. Don't worry. I know she's thinking about you.'

Raheem nodded and tried to put on a smile. His mum had moved to England a few months ago and he really missed her. She had promised that they would not be separated for long.

His grandmother finished the bedtime story, closed the book and tucked Raheem in. 'Night night, little man. Sweet dreams.'

'Night night,' Raheem replied. Before he turned off his lamp, he opened the drawer by the side of the bed and took out a crumpled envelope. This had become part of his routine lately. It was the most recent letter from his mum. He read it twice, kissed the paper and put it back in the envelope. He knew that they would be reunited soon.

Thousands of miles away in England, his mum lay awake after a late night at work. Nadine was tired but she couldn't sleep. Her mind turned to her children – and, in particular, little Raheem. What would he be doing at that moment? Was he missing her? Did he understand why she was doing it? It was the last question that troubled her the most. Raheem was still so young and she had struggled to explain why she was moving away.

But she just had to leave Maverley – for her sake and for her children's future. Every year, it became a more dangerous place with all kinds of crime and lots of local gangs. None of that was affecting Raheem yet, but what would happen when he was a teenager? It would be so easy to get caught up with the wrong group of friends. With the clock ticking, Nadine had made her decision. She would find a way out and make sure that her children had every chance of staying on a safer path.

Not that it was easy, of course. Tears had streamed down her face as she waved goodbye to Raheem and it felt as if she had cried throughout the whole flight to England. But once she landed in London, she had forced herself to be strong. Everyone was depending on her. If she was going to create this new life, she needed to find a job and a place to live.

Things had fallen into place quickly. She had found a vacancy on St Raphael's housing estate in north-west London straightaway and a hospital job nearby. She then began to put money aside into a white envelope, ready for bringing her family to London as soon as possible. Months later, the envelope was starting to bulge.

Thinking about Raheem always made her smile. He was such a cheeky little boy, full of energy and love. She reached for the notepad on the floor next to her bed. 'Time for another letter,' she said quietly. 'It won't be long until I have good news to share.'

CHAPTER 3

LEAVING THE SUN BEHIND

One morning, as he sat down in his usual chair for breakfast, Raheem's world was turned upside down. His grandmother gave him a sad smile and ran her fingers through his hair.

'Raheem, your mum called last night. She's been making plans. You're going to join her in England.'

Raheem looked confused. He didn't know where England was, or if he would still be able to meet up with his friends. He had so many questions but before he could launch into the list, his grandmother was giving him a plate of plantain and telling him more about the move.

'You leave in two weeks. That means you need to

start thinking about everything you want to pack. I'll give you one of my suitcases and we can pack it together. Then you're going on an airplane.'

Raheem's eyes widened. He had seen airplanes on television and he even had a toy plane that his grandmother had bought him last year for his birthday.

'Your mum has a place for you to live in London, the capital of England. She says there are lots of other boys in the neighbourhood. I'm sure you'll make lots of new friends.'

'I like the friends I have now.'

His grandmother paused. She had expected this. Raheem spent so much time with Christopher, Leon and the other boys who lived on their street. She wanted to make this move as easy as possible, but Raheem would be crushed to find out that he might never see his Maverley friends again.

'I know,' she replied. 'But football is even bigger in England. Your mum said it's all anyone ever talks about. There will leagues for you to join and coaches to help you get even better.'

Raheem shrugged. This was all happening so fast. He was excited that he would see his mum. He missed her. But England? He didn't know what to think.

'What school will I go to? Can I bring my football? How will we know where to meet Mum?' He was talking faster than ever as new thoughts popped into his head.

His grandmother walked over to him and put a hand on his shoulder. 'Raheem, I don't have all the answers. But I promise you one thing: everything will be OK.'

Raheem heard footsteps in the hallway. 'And I'll be with you to make sure everything is OK, little man,' a cheerful voice called. His sister, Lakima, appeared in the entrance to the little kitchen. 'You can hold my hand if you get too scared,' she added with a smile.

'I'm not scared,' Raheem shot back, not realising that it was a joke and his sister was hoping for that exact reaction. 'Nothing scares me.'

Lakima came over and hugged her little brother.

Raheem tried to wriggle away but his sister's arms were too strong. Kimberley, Raheem's other sister, rushed in to join the hug. 'As long as we're together, we'll be fine,' Lakima said, patting his cheek.

The next day, Raheem raced into his bedroom after another afternoon of football in the street. A brown suitcase was propped up next to his bed, with a short note on it. 'Ready for you to start packing,' it said, in his grandmother's handwriting.

Raheem sighed. He quickly decided that packing was boring. He wasn't sure which clothes and toys to pack so he just piled everything into the suitcase, pulled down the top and sat on it to make it close. 'Grandma, I've done it!' he called.

Moments later, Lakima walked past. 'Raheem, you don't need to pack everything! Leave some of these things here for when we come back to visit. My teacher said England is cold and rainy, so you don't need all those pairs of shorts.'

Cold and rainy? Raheem didn't like the sound of that. Why had his mum picked England when she could have stayed in sunny Jamaica? That didn't make any sense to him.

When the big day finally arrived, Raheem felt nervous. He hugged his friends Christopher and Leon. 'I promise I'll write you both a letter as soon as we get there. Then we can plan our next match.'

As they carried the suitcases out into the street ready for the drive to the airport, Raheem suddenly remembered that he had forgotten one important item. He darted back through the house and opened the back door. Hidden away out of sight was Raheem's football, which had started off white and shiny but now had pieces of leather falling off it. He tucked it under his arm and rushed back to join the rest of the family.

When he appeared clutching the football and scampered over to put it in his suitcase, everyone laughed. 'Well, you couldn't travel without that, could you?' his grandmother said, laughing so much that she almost fell over.

Five minutes later, Devon, a friend of the family, arrived and the cases were loaded into his car. As they began their journey to the airport, Raheem watched all the familiar places whizz by and wondered how long it would be until he was back in Jamaica.

CHAPTER 4

LONDON LIFE

As the doors of the airplane swung open, Raheem was jumping up and down. 'Is she there? Is she there?' he called to Lakima who was just ahead of him.

'I can't see yet. There are so many people out there. Oh wait, there she is! On the right.'

Raheem saw her too – his mum. It had been months since he had seen her but it felt like years. 'Mum!!!' he screamed, running towards her and jumping into her arms.

Nadine couldn't remember the last time she had felt so happy. She hugged Raheem and held on tightly, kissing the top of his head. 'I've been looking forward to this day for so long. I've missed you so much.'

All around them, other travellers were finding their families or the taxi drivers who were ready to take them to their next stop.

'Let's go, kids!' she said, with a wide grin. 'We're taking the bus and we need to get our tickets over there.' She pointed to a small counter against the wall. Moments later, they had their tickets and were walking outside to the bus stop.

The first thing that Raheem noticed was the cold. As he stepped out of the airport, clutching his mum's hand, a big gust of wind made him stumble. He shivered. It had been hot and sunny when they left Jamaica. This felt like a totally different world. Not for the first time, Raheem was unsure whether he was going to like England.

'Raheem, you're very quiet,' Nadine said as the bus was speeding towards north London. 'I know this is a big change but you'll get used to it. You'll have so many places to explore.'

Raheem didn't reply. He was too busy looking out of the window and playing with his toy car.

He finally spoke ten minutes later. 'Will I have my own room?'

Nadine smiled. 'You'll have to wait and see,' she said, winking at him. 'There's a park just across the road and I'm sure you'll enjoy taking your ball over there and meeting the other boys.'

Raheem had cheered up by the time they arrived at St Raphael's. He walked closely behind his mum, both of them looking around at their new surroundings. Some of the neighbours were watching as they carried their cases up the stairs. One of them smiled and waved.

'Hi, Trudi!' Nadine called. 'Come over and meet my family later on. We're finally all together again!'

That night, Raheem lay in his new bed and thought about everything that had happened in the past twenty-four hours. This was a new adventure but a scary one. He hoped he would make friends quickly and that his football skills might make that easier.

Nadine stood in the doorway to Raheem's room, peeking round the door. 'I hope I've done the right thing,' she whispered to herself. The dangers and 'no go' areas in Maverley were no secret, but north London had its own dangers. She had seen some worrying things during her time at St Raphael's but she was confident that her family would be safer here.

Raheem didn't waste any time in introducing himself to the other boys. At first, it was just kicking a ball around on the estate. He found a few other boys his age and they were always happy for Raheem to join in. Any time that he had a ball at his feet, he felt right.

But when Raheem started school in north London, everything felt wrong. It was very different to his experiences in Jamaica and having to adapt was very frustrating. He tried to pay attention to his teachers but he found it very hard to concentrate. His mind would wander: usually he was either thinking about football or talking to his friends. But it landed him in trouble. Time and time again, Nadine was called to see the headmaster and was told about Raheem's latest incident.

'Raheem, you've got to listen to your teachers,' she told him on the walk home one afternoon. 'The school is running out of patience. Keep quiet and work hard. That's all I'm asking.'

He nodded, then looked at the ground. He hated letting his mum down, but he hated school too. Sometimes he was naughty – he knew that – but sometimes it just felt like he couldn't focus on what his teachers were telling him. Was that really his fault?

Things at school went from bad to worse. Eventually, the headmaster lost patience and Nadine received the call she had been dreading: Raheem was being asked to leave the school.

Nadine knew she had to act quickly, or else Raheem might spiral away from an education and into the kinds of activities that she had worked so hard to protect him from. 'I have to get this next decision right,' she told one of her friends on the estate. 'Raheem needs to be at a school where the teachers understand his personality.'

As she researched her options, the decision became much easier. There was a school that seemed perfect for getting Raheem back on track: Vernon House Special School.

CHAPTER 5

NEW SCHOOL, NEW START

'Are you nervous for your first day?' asked Lance, one of the many boys who played football with Raheem on the estate.

'Not really, I needed the change. My last school just wasn't for me. I'm looking forward to starting fresh.'

Raheem meant it, even if he was a bit embarrassed about changing schools. It was only temporary, until he could improve his behaviour in class. He knew he could beat his learning difficulties, just as he had learnt to beat defenders on the football pitch. He just needed a bit more care and attention than a big school could offer him. At Vernon House, there were only six pupils in each class, so he wouldn't get the chance to be naughty.

When Nadine dropped Raheem off at school on his first day, the headmaster met him at the gates and took him to his class. 'Raheem, this is your new teacher, Mr Beschi.'

They shook hands. Chris Beschi was used to moody kids who wouldn't take their eyes off the floor, so it was nice to see Raheem's big, shy smile. He knew immediately that this was a good-natured boy that he could really help. 'Nice to meet you. I hear you're a keen footballer?'

Raheem grinned. 'Yes! Do you play football here?'

It was Chris's turn to smile. 'Do we play football here? Yes, of course we do!'

Raheem liked Vernon House for many reasons, but it was the football that was closest to his heart. This was school and yet they let him do what he loved most for two hours every day. Sometimes it was just the pupils playing amongst themselves but Raheem preferred it when they played ten-a-side, with five kids and five teachers on each side. It didn't take long for everyone to become aware of his talent.

'Raheem, we'll have you on our team,' Chris shouted as they all lined up in the playground.

'Sir, it's not fair!' the other kids complained. 'Whoever has Raheem always wins – it's like having a sixth adult on your team.'

Chris loved watching Raheem play football. In the classroom, he could sometimes get frustrated when he didn't understand something. But on the pitch, that energy and frustration was converted into something positive and amazing. He never stopped working for his teammates, even when they gave up. With the ball at his feet, Raheem's eyes lit up and the smile never left his face. He could run rings round the other players and he had perfected every trick imaginable.

Not only this, but football also allowed Chris to see Raheem's true intelligence. He was always thinking, trying to find new ways of creating goals. He knew exactly when to go forward and when to pass backwards and start the attack again. For an eight-year-old, he had some great ideas. 'Sir, in the next game, I'm going to play through the middle,' Raheem told him after class one day. 'I'll get more of the ball there and it's harder for the defenders when they don't know if I'll go left or right.'

Every week, Chris took Raheem and his fellow pupils on a mile-long walk to take photographs of a building development for a school project. It wasn't just any old site, however, especially not to Raheem. It was the new Wembley stadium, still under construction. Every time he looked up at the massive arch and the huge steel structure, he felt a shiver of excitement.

'One day, I'm going to play in that stadium in front of thousands of fans,' Raheem announced to everyone. None of the other boys laughed – they knew he wasn't joking. It became the dream that kept him focused.

Playing so much football was really helping Raheem to concentrate back in the classroom. And in such a small group, Chris was able to build up his confidence about learning. 'A lot of that frustration comes from you thinking you're not clever,' he told

Raheem. 'But you are – you just need to believe in yourself like you do on the football pitch.'

Although his behaviour was certainly improving, there were still moments when Chris saw the youngster's wild side. Raheem was mischievous more than anything, but it was easy to see how he could slip into bad habits. Chris was determined to keep him on the right path to success. After one training session where Raheem showed both his dazzling ball skills and his temper, he told him: 'If you carry on the way you're going, by the time you're seventeen you'll either be in prison or playing for England.'

The words stung Raheem and he never forgot them. If those were his two options, he knew which one he wanted – and he would work as hard as possible to make that a reality.

CHAPTER 6

DREAMING BIG

The more Raheem played, the more he loved it. Football had become the number one priority in his life. Each day revolved around it. And with every impressive performance, he allowed himself to dream of making it as a professional.

His friends could not believe how easy everything was for him, whether it was a game in the street or a proper match (for the school). Before long, all the local boys knew about his tricks and flicks.

'There's nothing I can't do with the ball,' Raheem told Darren proudly one afternoon.

'Are you sure you aren't Brazilian?' Darren joked.

'You can call me Heemio if you want. I think I'd fit

in well with Ronaldo and Ronaldinho.' Raheem had first seen Ronaldinho's skills when England played Brazil at the 2002 World Cup. Usual school lessons had been cancelled for the morning so that all the boys could crowd into a classroom to watch the game on a big television. Even though Raheem was cheering for England, he loved the way Ronaldinho played and spent the next few days trying to copy the free-kick that Ronaldinho lobbed past David Seaman for the winning goal.

Darren laughed at the idea of Raheem playing on the wing in a Brazil shirt and teaming up with the stars to leave defenders looking silly.

'Those kinds of players aren't afraid to try things,' Raheem said. 'That's how the game is meant to be played. The tricks don't always work but it's entertainment. Even if it only works once or twice per game, it could be the difference between winning and losing.'

Raheem soon had another idol to learn from – this time at his favourite team, Manchester United. Cristiano Ronaldo was one of the club's summer signings. Ronaldo could make the ball do amazing things, even as he was sprinting forward, and he was only seventeen.

'He has so much confidence and he never gets scared if he loses the ball a few times,' Raheem explained to anyone who would listen. 'He's going to be the best player in the league. Just give him a couple of years.'

His friends laughed. Raheem was known for his bold claims – and he was often right.

At school, most of his class supported one of the London teams – some Chelsea, some Arsenal, some Tottenham and even a few QPR or West Ham fans. Raheem was happy to claim Ronaldo as his own hero and let the others pick their own.

Every Saturday night, Raheem would wait for his mum to fall asleep and then sneak downstairs to watch *Match of the Day*. He turned the television on and quickly lowered the volume. He watched the Manchester United games closely, paying special attention to Ronaldo so that he could copy the tricks in the street the next day.

That was how it usually worked. Raheem would see a clever skill on *Match of the Day* and then he'd practise it over and over again until he had mastered it. Next, he would test it in games on the estate. The end result was usually some bruised ankles but some spectacular goals.

One evening, Raheem was in an especially good mood. And that meant he was in unstoppable form once the game started. 'Heemio, play the through ball!' Ollie screamed. But, as usual, Raheem had other ideas. He darted forward, fooling one defender with a stepover and another by swerving to the right. As the last defender raced towards him, Raheem flicked the ball up and over the defender's head, then volleyed it past the goalkeeper.

He raised his arms in the air. To his left, a group of boys and girls from his school chanted 'Heemio! Heemio! Heemio!' Raheem smiled at that. He was becoming a local celebrity. Sometimes that meant the older boys tried to push him around – otherwise his speed could embarrass them.

Raheem was eager to play on a bigger stage, and

he wasn't shy about aiming high. 'Mum, I want to play in the Premier League one day,' he announced one morning at breakfast.

'Well then, we better make sure the scouts know where they can find you,' Nadine replied.

'I know I can do it. I just need a team to take a chance on me and be willing to give me a proper trial. Then I'll let them see all my tricks.'

Nadine smiled. It was nice to see her son being so passionate about football, even if he wasn't treating his schoolwork with the same excitement. But she was used to it by now: it was football, football, football in her son's life.

CHAPTER 7

COPLAND HERO

'Mr Lawrence!' Lakima called through the fence. It was getting dark and the Copland Community School football coach was collecting up the balls after a training session. 'You need to let my brother, Raheem, play – they say he's the best player on the estate!'

Paul Lawrence liked Lakima's passion but he hadn't even heard of Raheem. 'OK, what year is he in?'

'No sir, he's not at Copland yet – he's still at primary school. But he'll be coming here in a couple of years.'

After Lakima told him about her younger brother,

Paul told her that he would take a look at him when he joined the school. There were a lot of kids that came to him, each of them claiming to be the best footballer on St Raphael's estate. Most of them were good but not as good as they thought they were.

However, Lakima kept asking him and after the sixth time, Paul finally agreed. If she was that determined, then he had to see this kid play. 'OK look, if you'll stop nagging me every day, I'll let him join in. Tell him to come down to practice tomorrow night at five.'

When Raheem turned up with his sister, Paul couldn't believe how small he was. The boy was only two years younger than most of the Copland players but, compared to them, Raheem looked like a baby. He was very shy and didn't talk to the other boys as they got ready for training. He stood on his own and practiced keepy-uppies. He was certainly good at that.

But as soon as the practice began, Raheem came alive. Every time he got the ball, he dribbled round three or four players with speed and skill. He could be a little greedy at times but he had some amazing tricks and when he couldn't go any further, he would pass to a teammate or score a goal. Paul knew he was watching something special. Raheem was fearless, even when defenders used their strength to try to push him off the ball. The kid seemed to love the challenge of playing against older boys.

'Nice work, Raheem!' Paul shouted from the touchline, clapping loudly as the kid fired a shot into the net for a second time. If only he was a few years older, the coach thought to himself; this kid would be great for the Copland team. The smile never left Raheem's face while he played; Paul loved to see kids enjoying football that much. For the full hour, Raheem never stopped running up and down the wings. The opposition players were exhausted by the end.

'I told you he was good!' Lakima joked as the training session ended.

'He's not just good – he's incredible!' one of the team replied. 'Sir, how can we get him in our team? We could win the cup with him on the wing.'

'We can't, I'm afraid – he's too young,' Paul said, patting the boy on the back. 'Raheem, well played today. Your sister was right about you – you're the real deal! As soon as you're a student here, I promise, you'll be one of our stars. Lakima, make sure he joins the school in two years, OK?'

Raheem couldn't wait to join Copland. They had one of the best football teams in London. And from the school playing fields, he could see the new Wembley stadium being built in the distance. He thought of it as his home ground. 'I'm going to play there one day,' he told Lakima.

Raheem's football skills were the talk of the estate but he wanted to test himself against other kids at other schools. He knew he was ready and he wanted to win trophies. His mum Nadine was really happy – finally her son had a focus in his life. After some difficult years, Raheem was really improving in class and he was doing well at school. And it was all because of football – she used to hate the sport but now she loved it.

'Mum, can I go out and play for an hour please?'

Raheem would ask after school. 'Lakima can keep an eye on me and I'll be back for dinner!' Nadine couldn't argue with that. If it kept her son out of trouble, he could play football all day long.

When he finally arrived at Copland, Raheem went straight into the school team. After the first practice, Paul went over to him and shook his hand. 'Wow, you certainly haven't lost your talent!' The coach laughed. 'You're even better than I remember. It's great to have you here.'

When Raheem was still in Year Seven, he was the captain and star of the Year Eight team. 'We've changed the rules for you,' Paul explained, with a big grin. With Raheem cutting inside from the left wing and scoring and setting up lots of goals, Copland beat team after team and made it all the way to the Brent Cup Final. 'Raheem could play for the Year Elevens and he'd still be the best player there,' Paul told the school's headmaster with pride.

'Right boys, let's go out and show them how good we are,' Raheem said before the game, proudly wearing his white captain's armband over the school's blue shirt. Away from football, he was still very shy but on the pitch he was a confident leader. He could see that some of the players were a bit nervous about the big match; he, on the other hand, couldn't wait. He wanted his fearlessness to rub off on his teammates. 'We've got nothing to be scared about – we can win this!' he shouted, rushing around to give everyone a high five.

In the final, Raheem was man of the match. The opposition had heard about him and they tried to kick him at every opportunity but Raheem was just too quick and too good for them. He was the best player by a mile. At the final whistle, the Copland players lifted their star player high into the sky as they celebrated their victory. 'I love winning,' he told his mum that night as she came into his room to say goodnight. 'It's the best feeling.'

'Something tells me you'll be winning plenty more trophies in the next few years,' Paul told Raheem as they stood in the school corridor. They were looking at a new photo framed on the wall – it was a picture of Raheem lifting the Brent Cup, with a massive grin all over his face. The caption underneath read: 'Man of the match Raheem Sterling, who scored a hat-trick and set up the other two goals.'

CHAPTER 8

CATCHING THE EYE

Nadine had been told many times how much talent Raheem had and she could see how important his skill was in helping him to stay away from the gang crime on the estate. She could teach him manners and respect but she couldn't do everything.

'The more football you play, the better, that's what I think!' she told Raheem at dinner one night. Lakima rolled her eyes; since he'd started playing football, Raheem had become the golden child, and he always got his way. 'When you let off steam on the pitch, you're an angel at home and at school.' He couldn't have been happier to hear his mum say that. Playing football was what he loved most of all.

Raheem enjoyed playing on the estate with his mates but by the age of nine, he was ready for bigger and better things. He wanted to play proper matches on proper pitches against proper teams. He wanted to wear a team kit and win trophies. Clive, a local youth worker, started taking him to Roe Green Park to practise.

'You've got so much talent!' Clive told Raheem one evening as they played one-on-one until it got dark. He was exhausted; Raheem always kept him on his toes with his stepovers and nutmegs. 'If you keep working hard, you really could be the next Ronaldinho!'

Thanks to Clive, Raheem started playing for a local church team, Alpha and Omega, in the evenings and at weekends. They had a good youth side and it was the challenge he needed. Clive always picked him up from the estate and took him to the games. He always found Raheem waiting for him outside, practicing his keepy-uppies.

'Do you ever rest or sleep?' Clive joked. 'I don't think I've ever seen you without a football at your feet!'

Raheem quickly became the star of the team. He was still small for his age but that just helped him to take defenders by surprise with his tricks. They just couldn't take the ball off him. Clive watched with pride as Raheem scored goal after goal. Despite being the best player on the pitch in most games, he was always modest and his teammates liked that about him.

The only problem for Raheem was losing – he couldn't stand it. He had got better at controlling his frustration but sometimes he just couldn't help it. Word had quickly spread across the league about Raheem and opposition teams would be rough with him in order to try to stop him. They would push him and kick him in the back of the leg when the referee wasn't looking. Raheem tried to stay calm but if he wasn't getting free-kicks and his team weren't playing well, he would lose his cool.

It was Clive's job to deal with Raheem's disappointments. 'Look, you can't win every time,' he said one day as they sat in the car outside his home after a particularly bad defeat. Raheem hadn't said a word on the journey. 'Life just isn't like that. Sometimes you'll lose and you have to learn to deal with that in the right way. That's what sportsmanship is all about.'

'But they were cheating!' Raheem complained.

'That might well be true but things aren't always fair. Part of growing up is accepting that things don't always go your way.'

Raheem promised to think hard about this advice. He agreed that getting aggravated was a waste of his energy and talent, especially when he was playing so well.

Clive wasn't the only one paying attention to Raheem. Peter Moring, a youth coach in the area, had first seen him playing for Oakington Manor Primary School. He'd been amazed by the kid's ability – it was so rare to see someone stand out so much at that age. When he then saw Raheem running rings around teams for Alpha and Omega, he knew that he was watching something special.

Peter knew he had to act. He decided to speak to one of his contacts connected to the team. 'Tell me more about the little left winger. No one got near him in today's game. Have you had many scouts watching him?'

It wasn't a surprise that people were interested in Raheem but Alpha and Omega didn't want to lose their star player. Plus, the coaches weren't sure that Raheem was ready for the pressures of professional academies just yet. He was still a very raw talent and he needed to be more consistent. He was definitely still learning.

The reply was clear: No scouts so far, but Raheem isn't going anywhere right now anyway.

Peter grinned when he heard that news. When he wasn't coaching, he was doing occasional scouting for QPR. If he saw a particularly good kid, he let QPR know. This was one of those times.

He made the call. 'I've just watched a terrific talent. His name is Raheem Sterling. I'll send over all the details but you should think about getting one of the Under-16 coaches out to watch him before another club snaps him up.'

CHAPTER 9

RAHEEM PARK RANGERS

'Welcome to the Queens Park Rangers School of Excellence,' John O'Neill, the Under-16s coach, told Raheem and Nadine when he met them at the entrance. 'We're really glad that you could come down tonight.'

John had taken his friend Peter Moring's advice to have a look at the Alpha and Omega left winger. 'You won't regret it!' Peter had told him and he was right. One cold evening, John watched as Raheem dribbled past one player after another for ninety minutes. It was like watching a man among boys, only Raheem was one of the smallest players on the pitch. The kid had everything that the academy looked for in a young player: composure, desire, work-rate and, of course, lots and lots of talent.

After the match, John asked to speak to Raheem. Reluctantly, the Alpha and Omega coaches agreed.

'It's great to meet you,' John said, shaking Raheem's hand. 'You were brilliant tonight – what a game!'

'Thanks,' Raheem replied with a shy smile. He didn't feel very comfortable talking to strangers, even about football. Clive stood next to him, ready to step in and help if needed. It was good to have his support.

'My name is John O'Neill,' the coach went on, 'and I'm one of the youth coaches at QPR. We're always looking for exciting young players like you. How would you like to come and train with us?'

Raheem couldn't believe it – a Championship side wanted him to try out for their academy. It would be a big step up from the local league but he felt ready to test himself against the best young players. He couldn't stop smiling. He couldn't wait to tell his mum and his friends on the estate. 'That sounds great!'

Before the training session began, John showed
Raheem and Nadine around the facilities. Compared
to the changing rooms at Alpha and Omega's ground,
it was like walking around Wembley stadium.
Raheem couldn't wait to play on their beautiful
green pitches. 'We used to be a big club,' John told
them, 'and we're on our way back up to the top.
Youngsters like you are our future – with your help,
we can get back to the Premier League!'

The Premier League – that was where Raheem
dreamed of playing. Cristiano Ronaldo, Thierry Henry,
Ryan Giggs; he wanted to follow in the footsteps of his
heroes. He wanted to play in front of thousands of fans
who chanted his name. Queens Park Rangers seemed
a great place to start his journey.

With Nadine working evenings at the hospital,
Raheem would take the bus on his own from the
St Raphael's estate over to the QPR academy. From
day one, everyone at the club was amazed at how
good Raheem was. And how tough he was too; for
someone so small, he could really battle with the
big boys. He started with the Under-12s and was

unstoppable. He was involved in every goal they scored, whether it was a shot or a pass.

'I think we should start calling you Raheem Park Rangers!' Steve Gallen, the youth development manager, joked after Raheem scored all five of the team's goals in an important win.

Unfortunately, the other youngsters just weren't at the same level and Raheem was often on the losing team, despite his best efforts. He had grown up fast in many ways but he still found it very hard to accept defeat, especially when he had tried so hard and done so well.

'What more can I do?' he complained to Steve on the sidelines one day, with tears streaming down his face. 'I can't play in every position!'

'Don't worry, kid – you were great!' Steve replied, but he knew this couldn't go on. Raheem was just too good for the Under-12s and the club needed to do everything to keep their bright young star happy.

So when Steve took over as Under-14s coach soon afterwards, he knew straight away who he wanted to add to his team.

'Raheem, you're coming to play for the Under-14s,' Steve told him after another practice where he'd been head and shoulders above the rest. 'I think you're ready for the next level up. I warn you, though – you'll be up against some very strong kids who won't like you trying to do your tricks!'

'Don't worry, coach,' Raheem replied, with a confident look. He wished people would stop talking about him being too small all of the time. 'I can handle myself!'

'Coaches will think your size is a problem,' Peter Moring told Raheem very early on during his time at QPR. He'd lost count of the number of excellent kids that he'd seen come and then go just because they weren't big enough. He really didn't want that to happen to someone as special as Raheem. 'So you have to be so good that they can't use that excuse,' he added. 'You might not have the strength but you've got plenty of skill!'

Even for the Under-14s, Raheem stood out. He had a calmness on the ball that most kids just didn't have. Where others ran around like headless chickens in the centre of the field, he found space and moved with grace until that electric burst of speed. Steve could tell that Raheem was really thinking on the pitch; his head was always up, looking for the best way to create a goal. It was so exciting to watch a player develop like that. Steve just hoped that Raheem would stay at QPR long enough to sample first team football.

CHAPTER 10

THE KING OF CASSIOBURY PARK

With things going so well for him at QPR, Raheem was the subject of lots of attention. Tom Walley had seen plenty of brilliant young players during his many years as a youth coach in London. He had worked with future England internationals David James and Ashley Cole. In Raheem, he saw that same superstar potential.

'He's got that bit of quality,' Tom said to himself when he first saw Raheem play. With his experience, Tom knew he could help him to achieve his dream of playing in the Premier League. He decided to take Raheem under his wing.

At Cassiobury Park in Watford, Tom watched

as Raheem played with a friend. With jumpers
for goalposts, Raheem attacked again and again,
using every trick he had to take the ball round his
opponent. Every now and then, Tom shouted some
advice but mostly, he just watched with amazement.
Very few kids had such natural ability on the ball.

'Raheem, I've organised a five-a-side game for next
week,' Tom said when the boys had finally stopped
playing. His friend lay on the grass breathing hard
but Raheem looked fresh and ready to play again. 'All
of the best youngsters in London will be in one place.
It should be fun and I want you to be there.'

Raheem nodded with pride. He didn't need to be
asked twice if there was a game of football going on,
especially one where he could test himself against
the best. He'd be there, even if he had to walk all
the way.

When he arrived for the game, Raheem recognised
a few of the other kids from the school and club
football he had played. He knew how good they
were but he refused to let nerves get the better
of him. This was where he belonged and he was

ready to prove it. The pitch was in the back garden of former Tottenham and England midfielder Tim Sherwood. Sherwood was now on the coaching staff at Tottenham; Raheem knew that it was the perfect opportunity to impress a Premier League club.

Raheem came back week after week to play in these matches. He loved the challenge and he was learning so much from Tim and Tom. With them looking after him, he was destined for great things, just as long as he could stay focused on his dream.

The enthusiastic young player loved running when he had a ball at his feet or a goal in front of him. Just running for the sake of running, however, was something he hated. 'What's the point? It's boring' was his usual complaint. The worst part of training with Tom was the 'Dustbin Run'. Every week, he would make them do shuttle runs between two bins placed 150 metres apart. Tom would time them and record their results.

'Kids, stamina is crucial,' he told them when he heard their loud groans. 'You'll thank me for this one day. It's one thing to be able to run a fast fifty metres but it's a very different thing to do it again and again for a whole ninety minutes. That's what you have to do at the top level.'

The first three or four runs were fine but by the fifth, Raheem's legs felt heavy and he found it hard to breathe. It was like he was swimming through treacle. 'Keep going!' Tom would shout to encourage them when they looked like they were struggling. Usually, Raheem could keep going until he was told to stop but one day, he just didn't want to do it anymore. On his sixth shuttle, Raheem threw himself to the ground, panting.

Tom had a firm word with Raheem in the changing room afterwards. 'Look, I know it's hard and I know it's not much fun but I don't ever want to see you give up like that again. You've got a lot of talent but if the dedication isn't there, you won't reach the top. I've seen it a million times, trust me. Do you think Cristiano Ronaldo just stops running when he feels like it? No, he keeps going until he can't do anymore.'

Raheem nodded to show that he had understood.

He needed to make sure his attitude was right at all times; he hated quitting as much as he hated losing.

'Character,' Tom said, his favourite word. 'That's what the best players have. Character makes a career. Tell yourself that the next time you feel like you can't be bothered.'

Raheem learnt his lesson and kept getting better and better under Tom's watchful eye. Back at QPR, he had outgrown the Under-14s and the Under-16s. They were trying to keep their star player away from the spotlight, so that other clubs didn't tempt him to move. He loved QPR, but he was starting to feel like he needed a change.

'Mum, would you be upset if I said I wanted to leave QPR?' Raheem said at dinner one night.

Nadine was silent for a minute while she chose her words. She could see that her son wasn't happy but she didn't want him to rush into anything. 'No, of course I wouldn't be upset, but I want you to think long and hard before you make a decision. They've been very good to you (and this whole family) but if you feel it's time to aim higher, then I'll support you all the way.'

CHAPTER 11

TIME TO MOVE ON

Steve Gallen wasn't going to lose Raheem without a fight. So when he was aged fourteen, Steve had him playing for the QPR Under-18s. Raheem looked tiny next to some of the giant defenders he was playing against. But that never stopped him, even though some of them were three or four years older than him.

'Why would I be scared?' Raheem replied when one of his teammates asked him. 'I know I'm good enough to beat them every time. The only way they can win is by fouling me, and that's what the referee is for!'

With such self-belief, there was just no stopping

Raheem. Suddenly, he became a local celebrity, but not everyone on the St Raphael's estate was happy for him. Due to his busy football schedule of practices and matches, Raheem was spending less and less time with the friends that he'd grown up with. They didn't like it and when he returned from training on the bus one night, they surrounded him.

'So you think you're too good for us now, is that it? Just because you're a football star, you can't hang out with us anymore?' said one of the kids who used to call him 'Heemio' when they played in the streets. In all, eight of them were blocking Raheem's path, and he felt uncomfortable.

That night, he spoke to his mum about it. 'Son, they're just jealous of your success,' she told him. 'It's tough growing up on this estate – very few get an opportunity like you have to escape and chase a better life. And it's hard for them to watch you doing so well. But when you're playing in the Premier League, I'll bet they'll be your best friends again, asking for free tickets! Try to ignore it but let me know if you have any more trouble.'

Raheem didn't want his childhood friends to hate him but he also wasn't going to let them stop him from achieving his dream, especially if they were simply jealous of him. He knew that scouts from Arsenal and Chelsea, two of the biggest clubs in the world, were watching him play.

QPR knew his potential too, but Steve was determined to keep Raheem in the youth squad for as long as possible.

'Kid, we want you to sign your youth terms here,' Steve said in a meeting with Raheem and Nadine. 'You're the best young player we've had at this club for a long time and we all know that you'll go on to bigger and better things. But for now, I think this is a great place for you to be. We'll keep looking after you as we have for the last three years.'

Raheem talked it through with his mum and decided it was the right thing to do. Signing youth terms didn't mean he couldn't then play for someone else, but it meant that a club would have to pay money to buy him. That way, QPR would get a transfer fee for all their hard work in developing his talent, and Raheem would feel he had paid the club back for all their support.

It was very rare to see a crowd of more than one hundred people at a QPR Under-18s game. And usually there were far fewer than that – a few scouts but mostly just the young players' friends and family. With Raheem performing so well on the left wing, however, suddenly the numbers quadrupled. Word had spread about QPR's latest wonderkid and everyone wanted to see him play. Raheem didn't disappoint; he loved to entertain people with his tricks.

'How does it feel to be the talk of the town? We heard there were scouts from Man City, Chelsea, Liverpool and Fulham at the game last week. You need to get yourself an agent!' his teammates teased him. They were really pleased for Raheem, although they had no idea what they would do without him if he left.

A lot of people had come to watch but no one had made an offer for him yet. Raheem was worried that Premier League clubs might be put off by not only his size but might also be frustrated about his behaviour in the past. 'Baggage' they called it – he was from a tough estate and at times his attitude was equally tough. But he was still a child trying hard to learn how to be an adult. 'One of the top teams will take a chance on me,' he told himself in an attempt to stay positive.

Steve spoke regularly with Nadine to try to keep Raheem happy. They had a lot of respect for each other as key figures in Raheem's life, and they both wanted the best for him.

'I just think it might be time for him to move on,' Nadine told Steve. 'He needs a change of scene and I don't just mean QPR; I think he needs a new start, away from London. Of course I don't want to see him leave but Raheem has too many distractions around here, too many people who could be bad influences.'

Steve understood but he had one last card to play. He called his young star into his office the next day. 'Raheem, you'll be playing for the QPR reserves this weekend. Do you think you're up to that challenge?'

'Of course!' Raheem replied with a massive grin. He was only fifteen and he was going to be playing with proper professional footballers.

Raheem did well in a very physical game. He was exhausted when he came off the pitch and the next day he had plenty of cuts and bruises. But his only thought was 'I want to go out there and play again!' He was really grateful for all of the chances that QPR had offered him but he couldn't help feeling that his time there was coming to an end.

'Steve, I'm sorry but I need to go,' Raheem said after training one day. Steve could see how upset the kid was to be saying this. He had tried so hard to keep Raheem at QPR but he knew he couldn't stand in his way any longer.

Raheem added: 'I know that there are scouts watching me and it's time for me to move on.'

CHAPTER 12

A RED IN THE MAKING

When Lee Anderson saw Raheem play for the first time, he got straight on the phone to his brother, Mark. 'You have to come down to QPR straight away,' he told him. 'Their left winger is incredible. He's not a big lad but, boy, can he play football!'

Mark was a youth scout for Liverpool Football Club. Lee would often call him to recommend players but he had never heard his brother sound so excited. 'This kid must be the real deal,' Mark thought to himself. He needed to make a trip to London.

At the QPR Under-18s' next match against Crystal Palace, Mark saw straightaway that he wasn't the only scout watching Raheem. He had never seen so many people at a game at this level. 'This is going to be good,' he said to himself as he waited for the game to kick off.

Mark wasn't disappointed; in fact he couldn't believe his eyes. Raheem's height wasn't ideal but the kid had more tricks than a magician. And he had a good 'football brain' as they said in the scouting trade; Raheem knew when to dribble, when to shoot and when to pass or cross to a teammate. You could teach some of that stuff but the best players already had it.

'When he runs at defenders, that pace is frightening,' Mark Warburton, the Brentford scout, said over a half-time cup of tea. Normally scouts kept their thoughts to themselves about players but there was no point in hiding anything when it came to Raheem. Every club wanted him. 'And he's got end product too – for a fifteen-year-old kid, that's a winning combination!'

In the second half, Raheem was just as impressive. What Mark Anderson really liked was the consistency of his play. He'd seen so many quick-footed wingers who would do one nice thing in a game but then a string of bad things. With Raheem, nothing was a fluke; he could play great passes every time and he could put in perfect crosses.

'How does a kid that small have enough power to do that?' Mark asked the man standing next to him, as Raheem scored with a brilliant shot into the bottom corner. The man had no answer for him.

Mark went back again and again to see Raheem play – and he did something special every time. He was exactly what Liverpool needed but Mark wanted to be sure about his attitude. He worked really hard on the pitch but, just occasionally, there was a flash of frustration.

'Man City, Chelsea, Tottenham, Arsenal – they've all had scouts down here,' Mark Warburton told him when he asked about Raheem's background. 'But none of them have made an offer – they say he's too small with too much "baggage". He's not from the best part of London but so far he's doing a decent job of keeping himself out of trouble. There's no way he's coming to Brentford so I can be honest – if I was you, I'd take a chance on him. If you look after him well, he could be one of England's best players in a few years.'

When Mark Anderson heard that Fulham had put in a bid for Raheem, he knew it was time to act. He called Frank McParland, the Academy Director at Liverpool FC.

'Frank, how soon can you come to QPR? There's a kid here that you really need to see. You know I don't say this often – he's the best thing I've ever seen. He's got some rough edges but we need him in our team!'

When Frank saw Raheem's talent, he agreed with Mark's assessment. They started to make their plans for persuading him to sign for Liverpool. They spoke to Nadine and other people close to Raheem. Their message was simple: 'Liverpool is a great club and the perfect place for Raheem. We'll really look after him, keep the distractions to a minimum and help him to become one of the best players in the world.'

'Raheem, come up to Liverpool and we'll show you around our training facilities,' Frank said with confidence. 'I promise you'll love it there. Once you see what we've got and meet some of the people, you'll know it's the right move for you.'

CHAPTER 13

A WELCOME FROM THE STARS

Mark Anderson drove Raheem and Nadine to Melwood, Liverpool's training ground. On the way they talked about Liverpool's future plans and how they were desperate to become the biggest club in English football again. 'You can be a huge part of that project, Raheem,' Mark told him. He liked the sound of that.

As Melwood came into view, he couldn't believe the size of the place – it was like a city of its own. It was totally different to what he'd known at QPR. Mark could see the surprise on the boy's face. 'It's quite impressive, isn't it?' he said and Raheem just nodded.

At the entrance, they were met by Frank McParland, the Liverpool Academy Director, and Rafa Benitez, the Liverpool manager. Rafa was wearing his club tracksuit with his initials, 'RB', under the liver bird on the club crest. Raheem couldn't believe that such a famous coach was taking the time to meet him. 'Wow, they must really want to sign me,' he thought to himself. They all sat down together and Rafa took charge of the meeting.

'This is one of the biggest clubs in the world but we want to make it *the* biggest club,' he said. 'In order to do that, we need a mix of great, experienced players and the best young talent. We'd love you to come and play here, Raheem. We see you as the future of this football club.'

It was a powerful speech and Raheem began to picture himself in the classic red shirt, celebrating another great goal with the fans at Anfield. He could tell that Liverpool would be a great club to play for. He looked over at his mum and she looked impressed too. Rafa then took Raheem on a tour of the facilities.

Raheem had never seen so many football pitches in one place, and the gym was the size of a shopping centre. They had all of the best equipment, plus an amazing swimming pool. There were lots of physios there helping players recovering from injury. 'As you can see, we really look after our players here,' Frank said as they moved on to the changing rooms.

As they made their way along the corridor, Steven Gerrard, the Liverpool captain, and Fernando Torres, Liverpool's superstar striker, came walking towards them. Raheem was totally star-struck. He was in the same building as two of the best players in the world. And instead of going straight past them, they stopped to chat.

'Stevie and Fernando, this is Raheem Sterling. He's one of the best young players in England and we're trying to persuade him to sign for Liverpool,' Rafa told them.

'Nice to meet you, I've heard a lot about you,' Stevie said, shaking his hand. Raheem couldn't believe that he was actually standing next to Steven Gerrard. He wanted to touch him to make sure it wasn't a fake. The whole day had been an unbelievable experience. 'Look, you've got to sign for Liverpool!' Stevie went on. 'This is the best football club in the world. Just you wait until you play in front of the fans here – there's no feeling like it.'

Fernando spoke next, asking him how he was enjoying the tour. 'The facilities are pretty incredible, aren't they? This is a great club to play for.'

Raheem didn't say a word – he couldn't, he was tongue-tied. If Steven Gerrard and Fernando Torres were telling him to sign for Liverpool, then surely he should sign for Liverpool, shouldn't he? Liverpool was a very different city from London but this was a top club with lots of money, a great history and brilliant footballers to learn from. Going to Fulham would mean he was still close to home but they were unlikely to ever challenge for the Premier League title, or to play in the Champions League.

Raheem had made up his mind, or at least Liverpool's superstars had made it up for him.

'Mum, I'm ready to sign,' he said on the train back to London. 'They clearly really want me and I can really picture myself playing there. What do you think?'

'Son, it has to be your decision,' Nadine told him. 'I'm worried about you leaving home and how the change will affect you, but I'm your mother so that's to be expected! I liked that the manager and the players came to meet you – I thought that was a very nice, personal touch. I'm sure they don't do that for every youngster that they sign for the academy!'

His mum was right; it would be a massive change for him but his mind was made up.

Liverpool paid QPR £500,000 for Raheem but if he did well, the fee could end up being as much as £2 million. It was a lot of money for a fifteen-year-old. Suddenly, he was the talk of the football world. There would be a lot of pressure on him to fulfil his potential but Raheem was determined to become a superstar.

'In a few years, that will seem like a bargain!' he joked with his family.

CHAPTER 14

LEAVING LONDON

'Hi Raheem, nice to meet you. I'm Sandra and this is Peter. Welcome to your new home!'

In Liverpool, Sandra and Peter seemed like really lovely people, but Raheem could already tell that it would be very strange living with people other than his mum and siblings. As his new 'house parents' showed him to his room, he felt like everyone he loved was a long way away. He could feel tears filling his eyes but blinked them away. As soon as Sandra and Peter left him to settle in, he called home.

'Hi, son,' Nadine answered straightaway. She was glad to hear his voice. 'Everything OK? How was the journey? How's your new room?'

'It's a lot bigger than my old one but... it's not the same,' Raheem replied. He didn't want to cry or worry his mum. It would just take some time to get used to his new situation. 'It feels really weird not having you guys around. You will come and visit, right?'

'Of course! As soon as you know when your first match is, we'll be there to cheer you on. It's only two-and-a-half hours on the train.'

Raheem had found it really hard saying goodbye to all his friends in London. He would miss all of the football matches in the parks around Wembley and at Copland Community School. He had learnt so much there and he had a lot of people to thank for helping him to stay out of trouble.

That night, Sandra cooked Raheem's new favourite meal: mac and cheese with salad. His mum must have told them on the phone. Over dinner, they talked about him growing up in London and his love of football. The food was great and the couple made him feel right at home. Peter was a big Liverpool fan, so he was excited to have a future star living in their house. 'You said you play on the wing? Well, when you become the next Stanley Matthews, don't forget about us! A free ticket every now and then would be nice!'

Raheem laughed – he didn't know who Stanley Matthews was but he promised that he'd get Peter a season ticket if he became an Anfield legend. They watched a bit of television together and then it was time for bed. It took Raheem a little while to get used to his new bed but he was soon fast asleep at the end of a very long and tiring day.

The next morning it was time to start at his new school. Raheem used to hate school but since his days at Vernon House, he was much happier in class. Football had really helped with his concentration and he was a clever kid when he tried hard.

Sandra dropped him outside Rainhill High School.

'Good luck, Raheem! Hope it goes well today,' she shouted to him as he walked towards the gates.

It was always hard to start again at a new school but luckily there were quite a few other Liverpool Academy players at Rainhill. They helped him to settle in and being a really good footballer certainly made it easier to make friends with the other boys. Just like at Vernon House and Copland, Raheem spent every spare minute out on the school playing field. Expectations were high and he had a few things to prove.

'I read about you in the newspaper!' one of his classmates told him. 'Wow, I'm playing with someone who's worth £2 million!'

Raheem didn't mind the extra attention from the others and he knew that all their jokes were light-hearted. They quickly saw how good he was on the field and welcomed him into their group. Some even found out about his nickname and started calling him 'Heemio', which really made him feel at home.

Although school was going well, Raheem couldn't help missing London. Back at his new home, he spent hours alone in his room listening to music and thinking about his friends and family. He didn't regret his decision to join Liverpool Football Club but he wished that he had his mum and sisters around for support.

'We'll be up to visit next week, Raheem,' Nadine told him on the phone. She was upset to hear her son sounding homesick. 'You'll have to show us around. Are there any good Jamaican restaurants in Liverpool?'

Raheem had no idea – he didn't really go out very much. If he wasn't at Rainhill and he wasn't training at Melwood, then he was back at Sandra and Peter's house. They were looking after him really well and he was starting to think of them like his second parents, but he couldn't wait to see his real mum. He had a whole new life that he wanted to share with her.

Nadine enjoyed her trip to Liverpool but she was in tears as she said goodbye to Raheem. On the train home, she thought long and hard about the situation. 'I have a good life and a good job in London but I want to be near my son,' she told herself. 'I'm sure I could get a job up in Liverpool and the kids would quickly get used to a new city...'

By the time she phoned Raheem that night, Nadine had made up her mind. 'Son, it might take a little while to sort out but I've decided that we're moving up to Liverpool. I can't leave you up there alone at your age – you need your mum by your side!'

Raheem was over the moon at the news. He jumped up and down on his bed, and he had a huge smile on his face. With his family around him again, there would be nothing stopping him from achieving his Anfield dream.

CHAPTER 15

FEARLESS

As he began his Liverpool career, Raheem showed no signs of the pressure while on the pitch. He was still only fifteen years old and he saw no reason to be scared of anything. He was just starting his journey to the very top and he was keen to impress his new coaches. Before he'd left London, Tom Walley had given him some advice. 'That £500,000 price-tag? Ignore it – it means nothing. Just keep playing the way you've always played with that smile on your face. You'll soon be worth fifty times that much!'

Raheem's size was the only worry, but he knew he had the skills and speed to get around that. 'Plus, I'm stronger than I look!' he joked with his new youth teammates, some of whom were nearly a foot taller than him. Wearing the Number 7 shirt, Raheem started on the left wing. Even though he was right footed, he had always felt at home on the left. It meant he could cut inside to shoot or cross with his right foot. But he wondered whether defenders would start to figure that out, now that he was playing at a higher level.

It was another test that he passed with flying colours. When it came to football, he was just a natural. In game after game, he danced his way past defenders who were much bigger than him, twisting one way and then the other. Every time he got the ball, he took it forward without any hesitation, and attacking at amazing speed. Opposition defenders had no idea what to do with this tiny wonderkid. He was everywhere, running down the wing one minute and then drifting into the middle of the pitch the next. It was like trying to mark a ghost.

'*End product! End product!*' – by now the phrase was stuck in Raheem's head like a really catchy song. He was never greedy; having beaten the right back, he then found the pass or cross to set up goals for others. Sometimes, Raheem even scored himself, although his shooting was something he really wanted to improve.

'He's absolutely fearless,' Raheem's youth team coach told Frank McParland, the Liverpool Academy director. 'They foul him and he gets straight back up and carries on. He jumps for headers with defenders double his size! You put a bit more muscle on that kid and he'll be one of Liverpool's best players in a few years.'

Frank was impressed by the glowing report and decided to take a look for himself. He had seen Raheem's skills back at QPR but he still wasn't ready for just how good he looked amongst Premier League-level academy players. On a pitch with twenty-one other bright young talents, he was head and shoulders above the rest in every way except his height.

For a fifteen-year-old, he had everything – hunger, pace, composure, vision, technique. His final delivery was strong and consistent, whether it was a shot, pass or cross. Frank had seen a lot of youngsters come through the Liverpool youth system over the years but very few had been this special.

He got straight on the phone to Liverpool manager Roy Hodgson. 'Roy, you have to come down and see Raheem play. He's the best winger I've ever seen come through at Anfield.'

For Raheem, it would be a life-changing phone call.

CHAPTER 16

TOURING WITH HIS HEROES

'Raheem, can I have a quick word?' Rodolfo Borrell, the youth team coach, asked at the end of training on a hot June day. Raheem nodded and waited behind as all the other players headed into the changing room. His legs were aching and he just wanted to get into the shower. He hoped that whatever Rodolfo had to tell him would be worth the wait.

'Frank McParland came down to have a look at you a month ago,' the coach said, 'and he told Roy Hodgson to come and take a look too. Roy was impressed and he wants to take you on the summer tour. It's a really good chance for the youngsters to see what playing with the first team is like.

Switzerland and Germany – three games in two weeks. How does that sound?'

'Amazing!' Raheem replied with a massive smile. His heart skipped a beat and he started to imagine the exciting moments that lay ahead. He'd be travelling with senior players like Jamie Carragher, Joe Cole and, of course, Steven Gerrard. He might not play for many minutes, but it would be an amazing opportunity to train with them and learn from them. And impress them with his talent. He couldn't wait to share the big news.

'Mum, I'm going on the Liverpool summer tour! Roy Hodgson's been watching me play and he wants me to go with all of the top players!'

'Raheem, that's brilliant! They must be very impressed with you. Can you believe how far you've come in the last few years?! Where is the tour going?'

'Switzerland and Germany. It's only two weeks.'

'OK, well, promise me you'll behave yourself.'

'Yes, Mum!' he said, rolling his eyes.

It was a great experience travelling with the

senior team. Once they'd seen Raheem in action, the players quickly welcomed him into the group. 'Playing against you makes me want to retire!' Jamie Carragher joked, as he stood panting, after chasing him down the wing.

When Raheem got a bit too cheeky with his dribbling in practice, Jamie and Steven Gerrard stopped him with strong tackles. He was playing with the big boys now and they didn't want to be shown up by the new wonderkid. Raheem learnt to keep things simple, and never complained. After all, he wasn't a star yet.

Raheem saw how good the top professionals were up close, how hard they all worked in training and how much effort he would need to put in to get to that level. 'Every training session is at such a high level,' he told his mum on the phone one night. 'The other players hardly ever make mistakes, but that's just pushing me to get better. I want to show that I belong at this level.'

Getting into the Liverpool first team squad was his next aim and he wanted to get there as soon as possible. But there were lots of really good youngsters like Tom Ince, Jay Spearing and Jonjo Shelvey who were ahead of him in the queue. He'd have to wait his turn. He had to watch from the sidelines as Liverpool drew against Grasshopper Club Zürich in Switzerland, and then lost against Kaiserslautern in Germany.

'Be patient, kid. I remember being your age and itching to get out on that pitch,' Glen Johnson told Raheem after the second match of the tour. He could see that he was disappointed to have been left on the bench. 'Keep impressing in the youth teams and the reserves and I think you'll be playing with us regularly before you know it.'

In the third and final match, against Borussia Mönchengladbach, and with about five minutes to go, Raheem finally got his opportunity. Liverpool were losing 1-0 but there was enough time left for him to try to make his mark. As he ran on to replace Jonjo, he puffed out his chest and prepared to do what he did best: attack. He did well during his brief performance but the team couldn't find an equaliser.

As he left the pitch, he was sad to lose but pleased with his personal progress. Sometimes he had to remind himself that he was still only fifteen.

Raheem had enjoyed his glimpse of playing at the top level and he was hungry for more. As the squad boarded the plane to return home, he was already thinking about the months ahead. He couldn't wait for the youth team season to start so he could prove that he deserved to move up to the first team on a permanent basis.

CHAPTER 17

YOUTH TEAM SUPERSTAR

'So how was it?' That was the question all Raheem's teammates were asking when he got back to training. One local lad who asked him was Conor Coady, who dreamed of playing for Liverpool in the Premier League. Conor was already England's Under-19s captain, so it was only a matter of time, but he was still pretty jealous that his mate had gone on the tour without him.

'It was brilliant,' Raheem replied. 'Those players are so good! I was a bit scared at first and they teased me a bit about being so young, but they're really nice guys and were really helpful. I can't wait to play in the first team!'

'Me neither!' Conor agreed.

'But for now, we've got the Premier Academy League and the Youth Cup to win!' Raheem said loudly, so that everyone else in the changing room could hear. 'Yeah!' was the response from his teammates around him. They were a good group of players and there was a strong team spirit. With Conor in midfield, Raheem on the wing and Michael Ngoo and Adam Morgan up front, they had a good chance of winning lots of matches.

The Liverpool Academy Under-18s were unbeaten until their sixth match of the season. Raheem found it so much fun playing in such an exciting team where everyone worked really well together. The team was scoring two or three goals in every game, and Raheem was at the heart of all the attacking play. In the game against Leeds United, he managed to score both of the goals himself.

His reward was a call-up to the England Under-17s for matches against Sweden, Georgia and Poland.

'I'm off to Georgia, Mum! I'm not even sure where that is,' Raheem told Nadine on the phone.

'You'll have to send me a postcard! You're really travelling the world these days!'

Raheem knew a lot of the other players from his time with the Under-16s, plus Adam Morgan would be going with him from Liverpool. It would be a fun trip and it was a real honour to be selected. Raheem started all three games and while he didn't score, he was happy with his performances. Just as at club level, he was getting closer to the big time with every game.

But it was time to get back to Liverpool. After a couple of defeats in the academy league, they had thumped Bolton 6-0, and now had a big Merseyside derby looming in a few days.

'We're doing well but we've got to beat Everton!' Conor said as they looked at the academy league table.

'Don't worry – we'll thrash them!' Raheem said with a big smile on his face.

In the end, though, it was a tense draw that left the two sides neck and neck at the top of Group C.

Liverpool and Raheem started 2011 in incredible form. He scored one goal against Manchester City and then, in one of his best ever games, achieved five against Southend in a 9-0 FA Youth Cup victory. He was simply unstoppable. For the first of his five, he used his pace to chase down a long goal-kick and shoot past the goalkeeper. For the next, he dribbled in from the left wing, past defender after defender, before smashing the ball into the top corner. To complete his hat-trick, he cut in onto his right foot in the penalty area and found the corner again.

'Man, when did your shooting get so good?' Conor shouted as they celebrated the goal.

'Practice makes perfect. Oh, and God-given talent, of course!' Raheem joked back.

In the second half, he did it all over again. Every time he got the ball, Southend's right-back looked terrified, flapping his arms desperately for others to help. Raheem ran between two defenders like they weren't even there, then past another one, before finding the bottom corner with a brilliant shot. He raced over to the touchline to celebrate and showed off with a little dance that his teammates copied.

And there was still time for one more goal. This

time, Raheem got the ball on the right wing and terrorised Southend's left-back for a change. He twisted one way and then the other, and found the far corner perfectly. Everything he kicked seemed to be hitting the back of the net.

Raheem made the sign of the cross, then kissed his hand and pointed towards to the skies. He had to thank God for performances like that.

'My five goal hero!' Nadine called out as she ran to greet her son after the game.

'Mum! Don't embarrass me in front of my mates,' Raheem replied, looking quickly over his shoulder. But he couldn't be angry on a day like this. He would never forget the day he scored five goals.

Word spread at Liverpool about Raheem's man of the match display. He was already the next big thing at Anfield but now he was the next *really* big thing. 'I think they'll want you in the first team soon,' Conor said, patting Raheem on the back. Raheem knew how competitive youth teams could be with so many boys fighting to keep their places, but he knew Conor was genuinely happy for him.

And Conor was right about the first team call-up. Liverpool manager Kenny Dalglish included Raheem in his twenty-three-man squad for Liverpool's Europa League match in February 2011 against AC Sparta Prague.

'Mum, I'm off to the Czech Republic with the senior squad!'

'Wow! Another country to add to your collection. But wait, what about school?'

'It's half-term, so there's no problem!' he replied quickly. Not that it really mattered. Deep down, he knew that school or no school, nothing would have stopped him going.

In the end, Raheem didn't make the bench for the match but it was a great experience to be around the senior players again. Step by step, he was working his way towards the Premier League.

When Raheem returned to the youth team, coach Rodolfo Borrell took care to make sure the promising player kept his feet on the ground. 'Seeing as you've had a little holiday, you can set out the cones for training.' Rodolfo had seen so many players get too confident about success at a young age. He didn't want that to happen to Raheem; he had so much potential and he wanted to protect that.

'Raheem, you've got to work harder there,' he shouted from the sidelines during the practice game. 'Just because you're an attacker, doesn't mean you don't have to defend!'

Raheem was angry at first. 'Why is he picking on me?' he asked Conor. But he soon understood what his coach was trying to do. There was plenty of hard work still to be done before he became a star. He showed his focus was still in the right place by scoring two more goals against Stoke City and then another against Huddersfield.

All in all, February 2011 had been a massive month for Raheem, and Rodolfo was the first to congratulate him. 'I'm really impressed by the way you've handled these last few weeks. You haven't let the talk go to your head. Well done, lad.'

CHAPTER 18

ENGLAND YOUNG GUN

The 2010–11 academy season was over and the Liverpool Under-18s had finished second in their league, just one point behind local rivals Everton. It had been a frustrating end to the season, so the boys really needed some good news, and as they arrived for a training session, Adam revealed what all the boys needed to hear. 'Raheem, we're in!' he shouted. 'We're all off to Mexico!'

In total, Liverpool had six players in the England squad for the FIFA Under-17 World Cup. Raheem couldn't wait – what an adventure it would be and what a chance to make a name for himself. At the 2009 tournament, Isco and Mario Götze had been

among the star players; back in 2007, it was Toni
Kroos and Danny Welbeck. Could it be Raheem in
2011?

'The pressure is on now, boys,' the head coach,
John Peacock, told them all when they arrived at the
training camp. From the very start, he wanted his
players to know that this was no holiday. 'We're one
of the favourites to win this. Last year, the England
Under-17s won the European Championships. I
know most of you weren't in the squad back then,
but we're still the best team in Europe. So don't let
me down.'

Raheem was ready to take this tournament very
seriously. In the group stages, England would play
Uruguay, Canada and Rwanda. England were
expected to beat all of these teams but in the
summer heat it would be tricky. Raheem knew his
speed would be a key weapon.

In the first match against Rwanda, it took
England nearly seventy minutes to take the lead.
Then, with only a few minutes left in the game,
Raheem got the ball on the left. He was still a

long way away from goal but he was never short
of confidence when it came to shooting. Plus,
everyone was expecting him to dribble... With a
defender coming towards him, Raheem curled the
ball up, up and over the goalkeeper and into the
top corner. What a goal! It was definitely one of the
best that he'd ever scored. Raheem celebrated by
performing the dance that he had practised with
teammate Nathaniel Chalobah.

'What a strike!' Kenny Swain, England's assistant
coach, said at the final whistle. He had always
predicted that Raheem would be one of their stars.
Defenders just didn't know what he'd do next.

After a disappointing 2-2 draw with Canada,
Raheem was rested for the final group match against
Uruguay. He was desperate to play but he knew
it was only fair to give all of the squad some game
time. His teammates won 2-0 without him to set up
a tie with England's arch enemies Argentina in the
next round. There was no way Raheem was sitting
on the bench for that one.

In the event, Argentina took an early lead but

England were always still in the game, especially with Raheem on the wing. With the first half coming to an end, he got the ball on the left. With a burst of speed he cut inside and fired it low and hard towards the far corner of the goal. It was a perfect shot that went beyond the goalkeeper's fingertips and into the bottom corner. 'Raheem to the rescue again!' Kenny shouted from the touchline as they celebrated. In the end the match went to penalties, and Raheem watched nervously as his teammates won 4-2.

'That's revenge for the shoot-out we lost to them at World Cup 1998!' Nathaniel joked after scoring the winning penalty.

In the quarter-finals, Raheem and his teammates faced England's other arch enemies, Germany. 'It's time for revenge for Euro 1996 now!' captain Nathaniel had told them before the game.

'Most of us weren't even two years old when that happened!' Raheem replied with a smile.

In the end, though, Germany were the better side and won 3-2, despite a good second-half fightback from England. It had been a good tournament for Raheem and he was proud of what he had achieved – two goals and some impressive performances. Now, he needed to carry on his good work back at Liverpool.

CHAPTER 19

THE NEXTGEN SERIES

Raheem was confused. 'What's this NextGen Series?' he asked Conor one day as they looked at the fixture list for the new season.

'It's a new tournament,' his mate replied. 'They say it's like the Champions League but for the youth teams. Barcelona, Ajax and Inter Milan have all got teams involved.'

Raheem liked the sound of that; he loved watching the Champions League, with the brilliant theme tune and the amazing players on display. The best against the best – that was the kind of tournament he wanted to play in. It was all about challenging himself.

'Great! Hopefully we can get out of our group,' Raheem said, already thinking ahead. 'I know the Portuguese youth teams are always really good but we should beat Molde and Wolfsburg.'

'Yeah, Sporting Lisbon will be really tough. That's where Cristiano Ronaldo played!'

Raheem's ears always pricked up when someone talked about his idol. He didn't think he'd ever be able to hit powerful free-kicks like Cristiano but he was working hard on improving his weaker left foot. Raheem loved the way the Portugal star was just as comfortable on both sides – it made it so much harder to defend against him.

Their first game took place in August 2011 at Anfield. Up against Sporting Lisbon, Liverpool put out a strong team but they were no match for the Portuguese side. Raheem was the bright spark and nearly scored a couple of times but in the end it just wasn't their day and they lost 3-0. Even so, Raheem was really impressed by the style and technique of the Portuguese players – they made everything look so easy.

'Wow, this tournament is going to be a real learning curve for us,' Raheem said to Adam afterwards. 'This isn't Southend United anymore!' He had a bag of ice strapped to each of his calves – it had been a very physical game for him. Every time Raheem ran with the ball, the defenders kicked and pushed him. Sporting Lisbon had obviously marked him out as Liverpool's most dangerous player, and did everything they could to keep him quiet.

'Well played today, Raheem,' Rodolfo told him as they left the stadium, but he could tell that he wasn't happy about losing like that. 'This tournament is going to be exactly what you need – a real challenge! You're as good as these kids if not better. Keep playing like that, and the whole world will start noticing.'

Raheem couldn't wait for his next chance to shine in Europe: against the Norwegian side Molde three weeks later. He nearly scored after just a few minutes but the goalkeeper managed to tip his dipping shot over the bar. Raheem was everywhere all game long, setting up goals, hitting the post and then finally he was rewarded: he scored Liverpool's fourth with a nice side-foot finish, having sprinted past his marker to get into the box.

'That's more like it, boys!' Conor told his teammates at the final whistle. They all looked exhausted as they had a gentle jog to warm down before leaving the pitch. Even Raheem had to admit that he was tired. But it didn't last long.

'Apparently King Kenny's coming to the game tonight!' The dressing room was suddenly full of energy, with loud conversations about who he would be there to watch.

'Toni Silva and Adam have been doing well but I think it's Raheem they're most interested in. They've been watching him for months,' Conor said and most seemed to agree.

Raheem really hoped his captain was right. Either way, it was a great opportunity for him to play well in front of the Liverpool first-team manager.

'If I hear one more word about Kenny Dalglish,' Rodolfo began his pre-match team-talk, 'then I'm going to start dropping players to the bench. He's been here plenty of times before and you just haven't noticed. It doesn't make a difference – stay focused and play your normal game. You never know, he might be here to watch one of the opposition players!'

Despite his coach's wise words, Raheem still felt a little nervous as he went out on to the pitch. He tried to forget about Kenny being in the crowd but it wasn't working.

He had a golden chance to score the opening goal but he hit it straight at the goalkeeper's legs. He stood there with his hands on his head cursing his luck – and Kenny wouldn't be impressed by that.

Raheem fared no better in the rest of the game. His touch was poor, his passing wasn't accurate enough and the right back was blocking his attacking runs every time. Then Adam came off the bench and scored two goals to win the match – right in front of Kenny Dalglish.

Rodolfo could tell that Raheem wasn't happy. He hadn't said a word in the changing room after the game and he was still sitting there staring at the floor.

'Chin up, lad!' the coach said. 'It wasn't your best day today, but it's never about one game is it? It's about performing at the highest level over the course of a whole season and then a whole career. I know you can do that and I know I'm not the only one telling Kenny that you can do that. Learn from today and be ready for the next one. Trust me – you'll have plenty more chances to impress.'

In the NextGen quarter-finals, Liverpool were drawn against Tottenham. Raheem had wanted to play against Barcelona or Ajax but they would just have to beat their English rivals first.

Yet Raheem shone in the Tottenham game. From the first whistle to the last, he was always on the ball and did brilliant things with it. Again and again, he dribbled past two or three Spurs defenders and crossed the ball into the box, but somehow Liverpool couldn't score. It was so frustrating but Raheem never gave up.

'We're playing so well!' he told Conor at half-time. 'It's just a matter of time before we score one and once we've scored one, we'll go on and score four or five.'

Raheem's prediction turned out to be wrong; in the second-half, Tottenham took the lead. Raheem couldn't believe it – it was so unfair. He attacked again and again but it was like there was a curse on Liverpool's shooting. When the final whistle went, he felt sick. He couldn't have done any more – how had they not won the game? It was a cruel way to learn the importance of taking your goal-scoring chances.

A few days later, though, Raheem and his teammates were smiling again. They were back in contention, as Tottenham had to drop out for fielding two underage players.

'It's great that we're back in the tournament,' Raheem said to Adam as they trained for their semi-final against Ajax. 'But it doesn't feel quite right, does it?'

In the end, the game against Ajax taught Raheem and his teammates another valuable football lesson: the power of 'total football'. The Dutch side's flowing style of passing may have been a joy to watch, but it was a nightmare to play against. Liverpool lost 6-0.

'That's not how I wanted us to go out of the

tournament,' Rodolfo told them afterwards, 'but they were a very, very good side. There's plenty that we can take away from that game and work on. Boys, well done this season – I think we'll be better next time!'

Raheem had really enjoyed the NextGen series. He loved testing himself against the best young players in Europe. There was still work to be done on his strength and shooting but he'd played well in almost every game.

'I think I'm ready for the step-up now,' he told his mum as they relaxed in the garden over the summer. 'The youth team's been great but I want first team games now. I just hope Liverpool are willing to take a chance on me.'

Nadine smiled. It felt like only yesterday that they were living on the estate and Raheem was a little boy running from room to room. 'Be patient, son! You've only just turned seventeen. They'll play you when they think you're ready. You can't rush these things.'

Luckily, Raheem wouldn't have to wait long at all.

CHAPTER 20

BURSTING ONTO THE SCENE

'Raheem, I've got some news you might want to hear,' Rodolfo shouted across the football pitch. His young star was still practising his shooting nearly an hour after the end of training. The goal was full of his successful shots from every angle. When he heard his coach calling his name, Raheem jogged over.

'How are you feeling?' Rodolfo asked him.

'Great thanks, coach. I'm feeling fit and healthy.'

'That's good because Kenny Dalglish called. He's named you in his squad for Saturday's game against Wigan.'

Raheem couldn't believe his dream was coming true. 'In the Premier League?'

'No, in the Rugby World Cup... Yes of course in the Premier League!'

Raheem felt dizzy. There were so many emotions. He was happy, excited, shocked and nervous all at the same time. His hard work over the last few years was really paying off. Many people had doubted that he had the right attitude to make it at football's highest level – but now he would prove them wrong. His number one fan was the first to hear the news.

'Wooooooooooooooo!' Nadine cheered, almost dropping the phone as she jumped up and down. 'My son, the Liverpool star! I could get used to telling people that! You need to get me a ticket so that I can be there to cheer you on.'

Raheem would never forget the day of his Liverpool debut: 24 March 2012. Entering the dressing room and seeing his shirt up there alongside all of the others gave him goosebumps: '31 Sterling'. He took a photo on his phone and sent it to all of his friends and family. He was happy with his squad number but he would have played in a '999' shirt if they had asked him to.

'Enjoy this moment, lad,' Steven Gerrard told him as they prepared for the game. The excitement on Raheem's face had got Stevie thinking about when he'd made his debut back in 1998. Back then, Raheem wasn't even four years old. 'You've earned your place here,' Stevie went on, 'so now show us what you've got. We've all seen and heard really good things. Don't rush things but don't be afraid to run at their defenders either.'

Raheem nodded and thanked Stevie for his advice. He was ready to prove to everyone that he was good enough to play in the Liverpool first team, even at the young age of seventeen.

Warming up before the game, he was the first out on the pitch. He had never felt so nervous or excited – he couldn't wait to play. The noise of the Anfield crowd was the loudest thing he'd ever heard and there was a sea of red everywhere he looked. He just hoped that he could make them happy with his performance on the pitch. He loved to entertain – that's what he did best. As he ran towards the famous Kop End of the stadium for the warm-up, the

Liverpool fans cheered his name. They knew who he was – and what an amazing feeling that was.

Walk on, walk on with hope in your heart

And you'll never walk alone

You'll never walk alone

Hearing the whole crowd sing the classic Liverpool anthem was even better. Raheem felt the hairs on his neck and arms stand on end, and a little shiver went through his body. Stevie had been right; they really were the best fans in the world. For some reason, his thoughts turned to Maverley and his friends back in Jamaica. He wondered what Christopher and Leon were doing now and whether they would believe how his life had turned out since he moved to England.

At the start of the Wigan game, Raheem was only on the bench but it was still amazing to be a part of the squad for a Premiership game. He was sharing a dressing room with Pepe Reina, Jamie Carragher, Steven Gerrard, Dirk Kuyt and Luis Suárez. They were his heroes and some of the best players in the world. And if he was lucky, maybe he would come on and play in the same team as them.

With only five minutes plus stoppage time to go, Liverpool were losing 2-1. It would be a very bad game for them to lose, especially against a team that would probably be relegated. Andy Carroll had come on at half-time to improve the attack but they needed more flair, especially from the wings, if they were to score a second.

'Raheem, get ready! You're coming on,' Steve Clarke, the assistant manager, called to him.

Raheem had never felt his heart beat so fast. This was it – his Premier League debut. He took deep breaths to keep himself as calm as possible. As he waited on the touchline, wearing the famous red Liverpool shirt, Raheem felt on top of the world. It was his time to shine. He just wanted to get on the ball. At the age of seventeen years and 107 days, he was Liverpool's second youngest ever player, even younger than Anfield legend Michael Owen.

Dirk Kuyt gave him a low-five as he came off the field. 'Good luck!' he shouted over the noise of the cheering fans.

Raheem ran on slowly, taking his time. 'Remember

to keep things simple and controlled' – that's what Rodolfo had told him. He couldn't be greedy at this level. The first time he got the ball, he intended to dribble down the left wing but when he saw there were defenders ready to tackle him, he played the easy pass into the centre of midfield. Then he sprinted as fast as he could towards goal and nearly beat the goalkeeper to the ball over the top of the defence. Pace and skill – these were Raheem's key weapons, particularly against a tired defence.

A minute later, Raheem decided it was time to attack the right-back. He ran at him, did four stepovers and took the ball into the penalty area. He found Martin Škrtel but he couldn't get his shot on target.

But Raheem was pleased with his bright start – he was causing problems and creating chances. This was where he belonged. As he was Liverpool's biggest threat on the left, his teammates ensured they were getting the ball to him every time.

As he cut inside and ran towards the box, a Wigan midfielder flew in and brought him down. It was the

only way they could handle his speed. But Raheem
picked himself up and didn't complain.

Even though Liverpool lost, Raheem's exciting
performance gave the fans something positive to talk
about as they left Anfield. And there were similar
conversations in the Liverpool dressing room that
afternoon.

'Welcome to the Premier League!' Jamie Carragher
said to Raheem with a smile.

'You looked like you'd been playing out there for
years!' Stevie told him.

'As soon as you came on,' added Pepe with a
wink, 'those Wigan players couldn't wait for the
match to be over!'

As Raheem was leaving the dressing room, Kenny
Dalglish approached him. 'Kid, that was one of the
best ten-minute displays I've seen in years. If you can
do that over a full ninety minutes, you've got a really
bright future ahead of you. You'll be getting more
opportunities soon.'

Raheem grinned and his legs suddenly felt like
jelly – he couldn't help it. It was all happening so

fast. It meant so much to hear Kenny praising his performance. Despite the nerves, it had been an unforgettable day. He loved the atmosphere and the challenge of playing in such big games with millions of people watching. His mind was still buzzing and the smile wouldn't leave his face for days. He was already thinking ahead to his next aim: starting a Premier League match for the first time.

CHAPTER 21

FIGHTING FOR MORE OPPORTUNITIES

After such a promising debut against Wigan, Raheem had hoped to at least be on the Liverpool bench again for the next match against Newcastle. But with Craig Bellamy and Maxi Rodriguez back in the squad, there was no space for him anywhere. After a brief taste of the Premier League, it was back to youth team football.

'Don't worry, this is what usually happens with young talent,' Tom Walley told him on the phone. Raheem sounded very upset and frustrated about not being in the senior squad. Tom really admired the kid's ambition. 'They don't want to rush you, that's all. You're their new star and they're just looking at the big picture. They'll bring you on in a few games over the next couple of months. Then next season, you'll be playing a lot more.'

Tom had worked with lots of youngsters over the years, so Raheem was sure that his mentor knew what he was talking about. He knew that patience was not one of his strengths but he'd have to work on it, just like he'd worked on his shooting and defending.

It was over a month after the Wigan match when he next got the call.

'Raheem, you're in the senior squad for Tuesday's game against Fulham,' Rodolfo told him at training. 'Congratulations, Kenny clearly liked what he saw last time!'

Second time around, Raheem wasn't as nervous as he took his place in the Liverpool dressing room. The senior players were all really friendly and welcomed him back into the squad. They knew they'd be seeing a lot of him over the next few years.

After an early own goal, Liverpool were heading for another bad defeat. On the bench, Raheem couldn't sit still. He was chewing gum nervously and drinking from his water bottle every couple of minutes. He wanted to be out there playing and the minutes were ticking by.

'Take it easy!' Jamie Carragher said to him. 'You'll be on soon – you're our only attacking option left.'

As Raheem warmed up along the touchline, the Anfield crowd chanted his name. It was a clear sign that he was already a favourite with the fans; they wanted him out there on the pitch. After seventy-five minutes, Raheem finally came on, once again for Dirk Kuyt, and the crowd responded by giving him the loudest cheer of the day.

He did well on the wing, dribbling past defenders and crossing the ball for the strikers, but Liverpool lost again. It was two games and two defeats for Raheem; he wasn't used to being on the losing side and he hated it.

'Well played again today,' Kenny told him afterwards. He could tell that the youngster was disappointed. 'It wasn't your fault at all; it just wasn't our day.'

Raheem wasn't in the Liverpool squad for the
FA Cup Final defeat to Chelsea in May 2012 but
he faced them just three days later, for the Premier
League match against John Terry and the Blues three
days later. 'Lads, we need revenge today,' Jamie told
them in the dressing room before the game to get
them in the mood. 'They beat us in the cup, now we
beat them in the league!'

With Liverpool 4-1 up, Raheem was desperate to
join the party. Finally, with ten minutes to go, Kenny
brought him on. It was too late to really do much
but it was nice to be a part of such a massive victory.
'Next season, you'll be in the team every week,'
Jonjo told him as the crowd clapped the Liverpool
fans after the game. 'There's no way they can leave
you in the youth team!'

Over the summer of 2012, Raheem worked harder
than ever on his strength. His size had always been
his biggest problem but he was determined to make
sure that didn't stop him. If he was stronger, it would
be harder for bigger defenders to knock him off the
ball. He had a new Liverpool manager to impress,

too; after a brilliant spell in charge at Swansea City, Brendan Rodgers had replaced Kenny Dalglish.

'They say he learnt everything he knows from Mourinho at Chelsea,' Jonjo said as they discussed the news.

'His teams always play really nice, attacking football so I'm excited!' Raheem replied. At Swansea, Rodgers had played with small, quick wingers; surely he'd want to do the same at Liverpool?

In summer training, the players would often have a laugh as they got themselves ready for the season ahead. They'd see who could hit the crossbar from the halfway line, and goalkeepers would take shots at strikers. But from the beginning, Brendan wanted them to get serious.

'Last season, we finished eighth,' he said. 'With the players we have and the money we've spent, that's just not good enough. Things are going to change around here. If you're not interested in working hard and getting better, then you can leave right now. The aim this season is to finish in the top four so that we're back in the Champions League where we belong. To do that, I'm going to need you all at your best.'

Raheem liked the sound of Brendan's plan. He was training with the first team all the time now and one day the manager came over to speak to him one on one. 'You're young and you've got a lot of talent. I'm looking to play better football this season – more passing, faster attacking. You're exactly the kind of player we'll need for that. Stay focused and you'll play a lot of football for me.'

Of course Raheem nodded – that encouragement just made him work even harder. But sometimes he couldn't help acting like the teenager that he still was. At training one day, Brendan caught him messing around. When Raheem tried to defend himself, the Liverpool manager was furious.

'Sterling, you know what I think of your football skills but you have got to have the right attitude for this. If you don't, you won't make the most of that potential and you won't be in my team. If I tell you to do something, you do it. You don't act the fool and you certainly don't argue with me. OK?'

Raheem was really annoyed at himself. It was hard to always stay focused at seventeen, when you just wanted to have fun and enjoy your football. But he knew what he wanted: to be the best player in the world and to win lots of trophies. In order to do that, he needed to get serious. This was his opportunity to play in the Premier League and he wasn't going to ruin that.

CHAPTER 22

SEIZING HIS CHANCE

'Mum, I'm in the starting eleven for tomorrow's game!'

It was August 2012, and only the second game of the new season; Raheem really hadn't expected Brendan to pick him so soon. And especially not in such a big game – against Premier League champions Manchester City. He'd be playing on the left, with new signing Fabio Borini on the right and Luis Suárez up front. He was playing ahead of £20 million signing Stewart Downing. Wow, the pressure was really on now.

'Son, that's brilliant news!' said Nadine. 'I'm so proud of you.'

'Well, I'm going to make you even prouder tomorrow. This is my chance. I have to play so well that Brendan can't even think about leaving me out again.'

Raheem was so excited that night that he couldn't fall asleep. He kept picturing the game, with him scoring the winning goal. In the end, he turned on the light and read one of his magazines as a distraction. Eventually, he fell asleep.

The next day, he raced down the stairs. The nerves were building and he could feel the butterflies in his stomach. He managed to eat two slices of toast, then he rushed to the front door to check his bag for the tenth time. His mum tried to tell him a story she had heard from one of the neighbours but Raheem wasn't listening. The only thing on his mind was the game that afternoon.

His mum drove him to Anfield. Raheem sat next to her in the front of the car but they didn't talk. He had his headphones on, with loud music helping to pump him up. Traffic was light so the journey took no time. As he stepped out of the car and walked towards the players' entrance, Raheem could already hear Liverpool fans chanting.

City had the best defence in the league: England goalkeeper Joe Hart, Pablo Zabaleta, Kolo Touré and club captain Vincent Kompany. It would be Raheem's biggest test yet. In previous games, he'd been given ten minutes to impress but now he had to do it for a full ninety minutes.

'You'll be great, mate,' Jonjo told him as they warmed up. He wasn't used to Raheem looking nervous; he was normally such a cool character. 'They'll try to scare you with some big tackles early on but Stevie will be there to protect you.'

Raheem played football without fear – that was one of the things that made him so good. He just had to believe in himself as much as everyone else did. It felt extra special walking out onto the Anfield pitch as part of the starting line-up with the crowd going wild. This was the big time and he was going to enjoy every minute of it.

His first touch came wide on the left wing. Raheem ran at Kolo Touré, dazzled him with some stepovers and then delivered a great cross into the box. Borini was on the run and Raheem found him perfectly but he hit it just wide. What a start. 'Great ball, Raheem!' Stevie shouted to encourage him.

Minutes later, Škrtel scored with a powerful header. Raheem ran over to celebrate with the team; he was one of the boys now and he was playing his part. 'Get in!' he screamed. In the second half, City got better and Raheem had to work hard in defence as well as attack. Carlos Tevez twice beat him with some great skill but Raheem kept going. Yaya Touré (brother of Kolo) equalised but then Suárez scored a brilliant free-kick to put Liverpool in front again.

The game ended 2-2 and Raheem had played every minute of it. It had been a brilliant game, performed at a really fast pace. By the time the final whistle went, he was exhausted. As they left the pitch, Tevez came over and asked to swap shirts with him. Raheem couldn't believe it – did Tevez really know who he was? It was yet another moment that he would never forget. 'We should get that framed,' his mum said when her son brought the shirt home.

Raheem was pleased with his first Premier League start. He hadn't scored, or set up a goal, but he had done everything right and he had never panicked. He had given Kolo Touré a difficult match with his speed and direct dribbling, and he had helped the team out in defence.

'Raheem, that was a great first game,' Brendan Rodgers said in the dressing room after the game. He was very proud of the way his young star had handled the big occasion. 'That's the attitude I'm looking for from you – you gave 110 per cent for the whole match. You did everything I asked of you and more.'

The young player was so pleased to hear that from his manager. A lot of the players also came over to say 'Well done'. They seemed really happy to have him in the squad and could see how he would help the team. Raheem had taken a big step on his journey to the top. If he kept playing like that, he would become a first team regular. His mum had tears in her eyes when Raheem saw her after the game. It was a day she would never forget either.

The newspapers the next day were full of praise for him. One had the headline: '*Liverpool get a glimpse of their future in fearless Raheem Sterling*'. 'Cut that one out,' he urged his mum. 'I'm going to need a bigger scrapbook to save all of these!' Suddenly, everyone was talking about Raheem. People were even discussing whether he would play for England or Jamaica at international level. It was crazy after only one full game for Liverpool. Luckily, there was no way that Brendan would let the fame go to Raheem's head.

'Sterling, focus!' the manager shouted the next day at training as the youth joked around. 'You think because you played one good game, you can just do what you want? Stevie's played hundreds of good games and he still listens, so get your act together.' The message was simple: he still had plenty of work to do.

CHAPTER 23

TAKING THE BIG GAMES IN HIS STRIDE

There was no way that Raheem was going to give up his first-team place now that he had earned it. 'I may be young but I've got the desire and I know I'm good enough to play every week,' he told his sister Lakima as they sat watching TV.

'I have no idea but Kingston thinks you're the best!' she replied. Their little brother was now four years old and he was already showing signs that he would follow in Raheem's footsteps. Raheem loved watching Kingston practising his tricks in the garden. 'He wears his little Liverpool shirt with "Sterling" on the back every day,' she said. 'He won't let Mum wash it!'

Raheem laughed. It was nice to have his family

around him, especially now that everything was going so well for him. It had taken him a while to settle in Liverpool after growing up on a busy London estate, but life here felt pretty normal now.

Liverpool's next game was another big encounter – Arsenal at Anfield. Raheem was desperate to play and he was over the moon when he saw his name in the starting eleven again. Brendan was showing real faith in him.

Raheem played well again against the London club but Liverpool lost 2-0. It was a disappointing start to the season but they were starting to play some really nice attacking football. Raheem was working well with Luis Suárez. It would just take a bit of time for them to adapt to the new manager's plans.

'Keep your heads up, guys,' Brendan told them in the dressing room afterwards. 'This is just the start.'

Against Sunderland a couple of weeks later, Raheem got his third start in a row. 'This is what I need,' he told his mum, as they finished dinner the night before the game. 'With a run of games, I can really develop.'

Sunderland took the lead but Liverpool always looked likely to score, especially with Raheem running at the defence. When Stewart Downing came on, Raheem moved over to the right wing. He was happy playing anywhere across the attack. From the left, he could cut inside but on the right he could run down the line and put crosses in.

Raheem knew he had the skill to beat their left-back Danny Rose every time. Sunderland were starting to mark him with an extra defender but Raheem dribbled past one and then inside past Rose. It was a magical move and he made it look so easy. The Liverpool fans were going wild with excitement. Raheem passed to Luis but his shot was blocked. Liverpool were getting closer and closer to scoring.

Moments later, Raheem was at it again. He got the ball and beat Rose with a lovely double stepover. With great composure he looked up and saw Luis in the penalty area. His cross reached Luis perfectly. The goalkeeper saved his first shot but he scored the rebound. Luis and Raheem celebrated the goal together; they were developing a really exciting partnership.

'Raheem, that was brilliant play!' Stevie said as he ran over to join the celebrations. As Liverpool captain, he was always looking out for Raheem, helping him when he needed it and praising him whenever he did something great. He was really pleased to see the youngster getting better and better with each game.

And Raheem was named man of the match. He was delighted with his progress and thanked his teammates and his manager for all their support. He proudly put the bottle of champagne next to his bag but he didn't open it. He knew his mum would want to add it to her collection of special awards from his career so far.

'Raheem, if you keep playing like that, there isn't a defender in the world that can stop you,' Brendan told him, giving him a big hug.

'Now all I want is a win and maybe a first goal!' Raheem told Jonjo as they got on the team coach to head back to Liverpool.

CHAPTER 24

ON THE SCORESHEET

Playing with Luis Suárez was a dream come true for Raheem. Suárez made brilliant runs in behind the defence and he was always where Raheem wanted him to be when he was crossing the ball. The Uruguayan's goal-scoring form in the 2012–13 season was just incredible. Away at Norwich City, the Liverpool players could only watch and admire as Luis scored four in a 5-2 win. Raheem played his part in a couple of the goals but Luis was in a league of his own.

'That guy can win games by himself!' Raheem joked with his mum later that night.

'He's very good but he needs you to run forward

with the ball and play it to him at just the right moment,' she replied. 'Otherwise he doesn't score! Talking of goals, I think you need to score one soon...'

'OK Mum, I'm trying!' Raheem could remember the days when his mum used to hate football. But when she realised it was something that her son was very good at, suddenly she started taking an interest. And now she watched every game Raheem played and gave him advice as if she was José Mourinho! It always made him laugh.

She was right, though. For the Liverpool youth teams, he had scored lots of goals. It wasn't that long ago that he had scored five in just one match, against Southend United. Goals in the Premier League were much more difficult to score but as one of the team's three main attackers, he would need to start helping Luis out. Raheem knew his shooting was good but he just needed to work hard and take his chances when they came.

Raheem's first goal for Liverpool finally happened against Reading in mid-October 2012. And not only did he score, but he also played probably his best match for the club so far. With his new 'Mohawk' hairstyle, he tormented the Reading defenders from start to finish. They just couldn't deal with the movement of Raheem and his left-side partner Glen Johnson. Again and again, they found each other in space down the wing.

Raheem's first and second shots were blocked, and his third was comfortably saved by the goalkeeper. But he refused to give up and when Luis played him in on goal after half an hour, he knew it was his golden opportunity. Raheem sprinted on to the ball, took two touches to control it and then, just as the defender arrived to tackle him, he hit it sweetly into the bottom corner of the net.

GOOOOOOOOOOOOOOOOOAAAAAAAAAAAA AAALLLLLLLLLLLLLLLL! It was a perfect finish that Luis would have been very proud of himself.

Raheem slid towards the corner flag on his knees. The Liverpool fans were chanting his name louder than ever. This was the greatest moment of his career so far. Luis ran over to celebrate with him and they

hugged: 'You did it – your first Premier League goal!'
Only Michael Owen had scored for Liverpool at a
younger age. It was another achievement for Raheem
to cross off his list.

It turned out to be the winning goal and Raheem
played the rest of the game with a massive smile on
his face and his confidence sky high. It was tiring just
watching him as he ran down the wing again and
again, creating chances for his teammates. With his
pace, he only had to knock the ball past a defender
and he was in the clear. Even when the defenders
fouled him, he just carried on trying to get a second
goal to seal the win. 'That's the big game I've been
waiting for,' he told Glen as they clapped the fans at
the end of the match.

'Raheem, those Reading defenders will have
nightmares about that match!' Stevie said at the final
whistle as he high-fived Raheem. 'That's one of the
best attacking performances I've ever seen in the
Premier League.' To hear that from his captain meant
the world to him.

In less than two months, Raheem had gone

from a little-known youngster to one of the most exciting players in the league. It was an incredible achievement for someone so young, but he already felt like he'd been playing at this level for years. He'd come a long way from the day that he'd been asked to leave primary school. There was a lot to be proud of.

After the match, manager Brendan was full of praise for Raheem. 'He is a terrific talent but he has a good head on young shoulders,' he told the news reporters. 'We have been doing a lot of work on the training field, but all credit to him.'

Despite this, Raheem could hear Brendan in his head, reminding him to stay focused. It would be so easy to relax and get too comfortable having made such a brilliant start to his football career. But Raheem had big plans to go to the very top and there was no time to stop and congratulate himself. The football world was waiting to see what he would do next.

CHAPTER 25

THREE LIONS ON THE SHIRT

'They're saying that Roy Hodgson is ready to give you your senior debut!' Jonjo Shelvey said at training one day. 'He wants to make sure that you pick England over Jamaica.'

He had only been playing in the Premier League for a few months, but Raheem was a man in great demand. In September 2012, he had been called up to the national squad at the last minute for England's World Cup qualifier against Ukraine but in the end he didn't get off the bench. Until he made his England debut, Raheem could still decide to play for Jamaica instead.

He loved his homeland and he was proud of his

cultural background. He often went back for holidays to visit his friends and family there. However, when it came to football, England had always been his home. It was in London and then Liverpool where Raheem had received his football education. He had already played for England Under-16s, Under-17s and Under-21s – wouldn't it be strange to change his mind now?

Raheem talked it through with his mum.

'It's your choice, Raheem,' Nadine told him. 'I don't want you to ever forget your Jamaican roots but this is about football. When I chose to bring you here as a five-year-old, I knew that you would grow up thinking of yourself as English. So don't worry, I won't be mad whichever country you decide to play for.'

Raheem was glad to hear that; he really didn't want to let his mum down. And she was right – this was about football and it was England that had helped to develop his talent. It would be an amazing feeling to play for them if they picked him.

Back at club level, Raheem was playing every

minute of every game for Liverpool. He was relishing the challenge of the big games – first a Merseyside derby against Everton, then two weeks later a trip to Chelsea. Sometimes Raheem had to pinch himself to make sure that his dream had actually come true.

'How are you feeling, kid?' the physio asked as he did his tests at the Melwood training facility. 'You must be exhausted – playing so many top-level games is hard on a seventeen-year-old body.' Liverpool really wanted to protect their wonderkid from injuries.

'I feel great!' Raheem replied instantly. 'I don't need a rest. I'll be ready for the next game.'

In mid-November, Raheem got what he wanted more than anything: his debut appearance for England. It wasn't at Wembley as he had hoped, but that didn't matter. What mattered was stepping out with the three lions on his shirt alongside ten of England's best players. These included Joe Hart, Leighton Baines, Steven Gerrard and Danny Welbeck. It was a true honour to play with them and it was a match that Raheem would never forget.

Sweden's Zlatan Ibrahimović stole the headlines

but Raheem was pleased with his first international performance. He had been lively throughout and had proved that he was good enough for the biggest stage. 'Great work, lad!' Stevie congratulated him in the dressing room afterwards. 'You looked really comfortable out there tonight.'

What a year 2012 was proving to be, and it got even better for Raheem when Liverpool offered him a new five-year contract in December. It was the perfect reward for his impressive form so far in the season. Raheem was no longer a youth team player; he was now a first-team star for one of the Premier League's biggest clubs. He couldn't be happier with how far he'd come. 'It's every eighteen-year-old's dream,' Raheem told the media. 'I'm just really grateful to be at such a big club like this.'

With Brendan Rodgers's help, Raheem was determined to keep his feet on the ground. Yes, he was now earning a lot of money, but he was not a superstar yet. 'There's a lot more to be done,' he told the Liverpool website. 'As the manager has said, I haven't begun yet.'

Raheem was keen to start 2013 where he'd left off in 2012. Twenty minutes into the first game of the New Year, Luis played a great ball over the top of the Sunderland defence. Raheem was on to it in a flash and as the goalkeeper came out to close him down, he lifted it beautifully over him and into the back of the net.

GOOOOOOOOOOOOOAAAAAAAAAAAAAAALLL LLLLLLLLLLLLLLLL!!!

With over 40,000 Liverpool fans cheering his name, Raheem ran towards Luis and they celebrated together. Their partnership was developing into something very special. 'This is just the start,' Raheem told himself once again. 'I'm here to stay!'

RAHEEM STERLING'S HONOURS

Individual

★ Liverpool Young Player of the Year Award: 2013–14, 2014–15

★ Golden Boy Award: 2014

BIBLIOGRAPHY

Calvin, Michael, *The Nowhere Men: The Unknown Story of Football's True Talent Spotters* (London: Century, 2013)

Articles

'History boys: Dalglish to get teenage kicks in Prague with Liverpool starlet Sterling' (*Daily Mail*, Web: 16 February 2011):
http://www.dailymail.co.uk/sport/football/article-1357492/Liverpool-set-make-Raheem-Sterling-youngest-player-Europa-League-tie.html

Bernstein, Joe, 'RAHEEM STERLING INTERVIEW: I used to be wild off the pitch... now I go crazy on it!' (*Daily Mail*, Web: 13 September 2014):
http://www.dailymail.co.uk/sport/football/article-2754063/RAHEEM-STERLING-INTERVIEW-I-used-wild-pitch-I-crazy.html

Calvin, Michael, 'The Last Word: Sterling's road from
kid to commodity' (*Independent*, Web: 2 December
2012):
http://www.independent.co.uk/sport/football/
news-and-comment/the-last-word-sterlings-road-
from-kid-to-commodity-8373825.html

Collinge, Miranda, '8 Wardrobe Essentials For
Summer with Raheem Sterling' (*Esquire* magazine,
Web: 30 April 2014):
http://www.esquire.co.uk/style/article/6174/
raheem-sterling-style-interview/

Cross, John, 'Raheem Sterling interview: Mum's my
Mourinho… and Steven Gerrard is my Yoda' (*Daily
Mirror*, Web: 10 January 2013):
http://www.mirror.co.uk/sport/football/
news/raheem-sterling-interview-the-liverpool-
starlet-1528167

Dickenson, James, 'Arsenal, Chelsea, Spurs and Fulham REJECTED Liverpool star Raheem Sterling' (*Daily Express*, Web: 20 October 2014):
http://www.express.co.uk/sport/football/525036/Raheem-Sterling-Liverpool-QPR-rejected-Arsenal-Chelsea-Tottenham-Fulham-London

Gholam, Simeon, 'Former QPR scout reveals he received £50 for recommending them Raheem Sterling' (*Daily Mail*, Web: 3 February 2015):
http://www.dailymail.co.uk/sport/football/article-2937014/Former-QPR-scout-reveals-received-50-recommending-Raheem-Sterling.html

Jaffe-Pearce, Michele, 'A Life in the Day of Raheem Sterling, footballer' (*The Sunday Times*, Web: 12 April 2015):
http://www.thesundaytimes.co.uk/sto/Magazine/article1540494.